Reflections for Abundant Life

A Spiritual Devotional, Practically Speaking

Audrey J. White

Published by
Cross Words Designs, LLC
CrossWordsDesigns.com
Southfield, Michigan

Published by Cross Words Designs, LLC
CrossWordsDesigns.com
Southfield, Michigan
Email: contact@crosswordsdesigns.com

Library of Congress Control Number: 2026903298

ISBN 979-8-9946771-0-0

Cover design: JillZee Design

Cover image: Dreamstime Images

Interior design: Valerie J. Lewis Coleman of Pen of the Writer, LLC

Printed in the United States of America

The thief cometh not, but for to steal,
and to kill, and to destroy:
I am come that they might have life, and
that they might have it more abundantly.
–John 10:10

Dedication

I dedicate this book to Maria Simpson, who believed in
this from its inception. She encouraged
me by telling me, "I would buy that book."
Through the years, she continued to inspire me saying,
"Still waiting for that book."
Thank you, Maria; here it is!

Acknowledgements

To Jesus, my Lord and Savior, and so much more. Thank You for inviting me into relationship with You through the gift of salvation. I would not have known what life truly is or could be, were it not for Your rescuing me from a dead existence. Thank You for making Yourself known to me and for showing me that You are real. Everything changed as a result of Your love and grace. Although there were times when life was not pleasant or what I expected, it was all in Your hands and timing, and it was always for my benefit and for Your glory! Thank You!

To my family, I am grateful, not only for our connection as blood relatives, but more so for our connection as sisters and brothers, through the blood of Jesus! Thank you for your love and support!

To Pastor Lois Tyler, my pastor, spiritual mentor, friend and sister in Christ. Thank you for being a walking epistle and example of what the Christian love-walk is supposed to look and be like. Your wisdom, discernment, and guidance have helped me to discover who I am in Christ and to understand how to both overcome and endure difficult challenges we all encounter on this side of heaven. Most of all, under your ministry, I learned that I could have a real, personal and intimate relationship with our Lord Jesus Christ. Thank you!

To the Daughters of Zion Ministries and The Reconciled Church, my sisters and brothers in Christ and dear friends, thank you for your friendship, prayers, correction, help, understanding, love, counsel and encouragement. Thank you for accompanying me on this journey called life. You personify the verse, "God setteth the solitary in families…" (Psalm 68:6a). Thank you for all of your love and support!

To my BFFs, my "through-thick-and-thin" friends (A, B, F, M, S, and V, known as "the Hens"), thank you for 50 years of blessed friendship. You have been there for me in ways that are indescribable! I love you guys!

To my editor, Shairon Parks, you are a woman of utmost faith, integrity, and professionalism. Using your God-given gift, I am beyond blessed by what you have done with my first manuscript. Thank you so much for your patience, advice, prayers, encouragement and belief in this work. I am grateful to the Lord for placing you in my life to help me walk in purpose, all for the glory of God! It has been an absolute pleasure working with you!

To my readers, I pray that you are blessed by this book. My sincerest hope for you is that something in this devotional will draw you into a personal relationship with Jesus Christ, resulting in your eternal salvation!

Table of Contents

Author's Note

This book originally started out as a daily devotional with fifty-two entries.

"Why fifty-two days? Was there any significance to that?" my cousin asked me one day.

"No," I told her. I explained that the number represented the number of "ministry moments" that I had actually written, as opposed to sharing what others had written. However, a light bulb popped on for both of us!

Fifty-two devotionals—one devotional per week, making this a "weekly devotional" instead of a "daily devotional." That truly was a Holy-Spirit-led idea, which makes this devotional somewhat unique!

Each devotional entry is longer than most devotionals on the market. While I do enjoy daily devotionals, I sometimes struggle with them. I want time to meditate on (and remember) what I have read before going on to another one the very next day.

It is my hope that as you read this book, you will take your time during the week to reflect on and practice what you have received in each devotional.

Introduction

Life is funny. Many years ago, my teacher, friend, then-leader of our ministry, and now my pastor, gave me a gift. It wasn't for any special occasion, as far as I recall. It was just a small, personal gift. When I opened it up, I found a pamphlet of lined pages titled "Sermon Notes." I remember laughing and thinking to myself, "Ha, ha, very funny." I wondered why she would give me such a gift. I certainly wasn't writing sermons, and the idea that I might was even funnier to me. While the gift struck me as odd, it came from someone I loved, so I held onto it. Now, at times I have been accused of being a "dimmer bulb" – you know, one of those lights that is very dim when you first turn it on but eventually brightens to its full capacity after a few moments. I guess I am like that at times. After a few days, I realized that "Sermon Notes" was not for me to use for writing sermons; it was for me to take to church to record what the pastor was preaching! Ahh, I get it now.

But here is how life is funny. Many years later, I would step into the role of pulpit leader, bringing a short inspirational message before the pastor preaches her sermon. And even funnier—some years after that, truly unbeknownst to me at the time (but not to God), I would become a minister at our church. Receiving that gift so many years before, and my original understanding of it, were truly prophetic. Needless to say, I have ended up writing and giving the main message at our church, on occasion. Most certainly, I've found that pamphlet of "Sermon Notes" to be useful.

I am amazed at how God orchestrates our lives and how He knows the plans He has for us—plans to prosper us and not to harm us, plans to give us a hope and a future! Many authors of spiritual books begin by saying, "I never would have thought that God would call me to write a book!" I have the same testimony. While I have always loved to write, it never occurred to me that someday, I would write a book—let alone a spiritual one. It has been my joy to walk with the Lord on this journey that led me to writing for you this book of devotionals, born of the many experiences that brought me to the place of giving inspirational messages to our small congregation as a pulpit leader.

God has blessed me immensely in my coming to know, walking with, and trusting Him. Because of His grace, training, sculpting, molding, shaping, correction, humbling and guidance, my life has blossomed into something I at times don't even recognize. Every true child of God, every true follower of Christ, can surely say, "As I look back, I cannot believe how God has changed my life, or rather, saved my life." I can surely see His overarching, omniscient hand directing the course and path of my life, as the rivers of water, turning it whithersoever He willed. What a journey this has been!

The prompting to write this book came from people in our congregation who would come to me after a service and ask me things like, "Can I get a copy of your message?" At first, I willingly and readily provided copies to anyone who asked. Then someone encouraged me not to pass them out so widely, but to save and compile them into a book. I sensed a prophetic charge in that idea and quickly realized and hoped that God could use these devotionals to bless many people. As stated earlier, a special member of our congregation, someone who had once asked me for a copy of a message, provided the encouragement I needed to complete this book.

I was not saved as a child, as a teenager, or even as a very young adult. I accepted Christ in my early thirties. Having grown up attending several kinds of churches as a ritual—some Episcopalian, some Presbyterian and some not Christian at all—there was never any true meaning for me. It was just something that our small family did together on occasional Sundays and major holidays. I vaguely knew who Jesus was.

I was raised hearing biblical phrases and words I just didn't understand (nor could I; I wasn't saved). I didn't even know what "saved" meant. The first time a woman asked me, "Are you saved?" I looked at her and asked, "Saved from what?" I had no clue. Later, when I learned that Jesus cares about everything concerning me, even helping me—whether to find a lost earring or to pick out a printer or a furnace company—knowing this made quite a difference in my life!

After becoming a Christian, I was learning about God, but it wasn't until I was blessed to be part of a prayer and deliverance ministry that I learned what it means to be in a relationship with God. Of course, I knew and believed that Jesus was a real person, but I didn't know that I could be in relationship with Him, much less how. That ministry taught me that God is real! And that is why I have written this book.

The main thing people miss and misunderstand is that our walk with Jesus is all about having a relationship with a person. It's about getting to know the character and attributes of the triune God (one person, three distinct personalities)—talking with Him, listening to Him and obeying His promptings. Being in relationship with God helps you understand who He is and who He created you to be, so you can fulfill your life's purpose. It's not about going to church and/or doing great works, although those things are necessary parts of the journey. It's also about experiencing a relationship that surpasses any other relationship you could ever have. Jesus cares about every detail of your life, and He sacrificed His own so that you can have life and have it more abundantly.

Though Holy Spirit-led and spiritual, Reflections for Abundant Life, A Spiritual Devotional, Practically Speaking is written from a practical perspective to help us all come to realize just how real Jesus is. Jesus cares about both our natural and spiritual lives. That realization made a profound difference to me as a new believer. This book is written for any audience, but my heart especially goes out to new believers and to those who are curious and interested yet uncertain about seeking a relationship with Jesus.

The devotionals in this book are written to encourage, convict and provide answers where there might be questions. I want you and others to know that Jesus cares about you and wants a real relationship with you! It's in that relationship where you'll get to know Him and who you were really created to be! Jesus loves you more than you (or I) can comprehend, and He wants you to get to know Him. If you accept His free gift of salvation, He promises that you will spend eternal life in heaven with Him and will not be condemned to a life in hell. Hell is a real place to which those who do not place their trust in Jesus will go. God does not send anyone to hell; that is a choice humans make because God has given them a free will. His plan was that none should go there, which is why He sent His Son, Jesus, to die in their place.

Choose eternal life by getting to know God through a personal relationship with Jesus! God wants to fulfill you in ways you didn't know were possible. He wants to fill whatever role is missing or needed in your life: father, mother, counselor, provider, husband, wife, friend and so much more. God has great things in store for you: to make your life over and blossom you into the beautiful creation He originally had in mind and heart.

I have prayed that this book will bless you and that you will come to know the *real* God, in three persons, and friend whom I have come to know!

Week 1

How to Live Life: Taking a Lesson from Birds

I have been listening to birds sing outside my window. I have been watching them a little and meditating on them. One day, the Lord gave me these observations.

We can learn a lot from birds, as evidenced in the Word. For one, birds live a simple life—the one their Creator designed for them. They arise early in the morning and begin their day in worship by singing to their Creator.

> *But I will sing of Your power; Yes, I will sing aloud of Your mercy in the morning;*
> –Psalm 59:16a NKJV

> *It is good to give thanks to the LORD, And to sing praises to Your name, O Most High; To declare Your lovingkindness in the morning, And Your faithfulness every night.*
> –Psalm 92:1-2 NKJV

> *I love them that love me; and those that seek me early shall find me.*
> –Proverbs 8:17

> "A bird does not sing because it has an answer. It sings because it has a song."
>
> –Joan Walsh Anglund, 1967

What I got from that is that everything may not seem or appear to be going right in our lives, and we may not be able to figure everything out; however, we can praise and worship our Lord by singing our song to Him.

Birds eat simply as the Lord provides for them. They are not preoccupied with food, and they seem to be satisfied. Have you ever seen a bird that looks undernourished? Or one that appears to be overweight? Also, birds basically have one outfit; they're not concerned about what they will wear.

> *"Therefore I say to you, do not worry about your life, what you will eat or what you will drink; nor about your body, what you will put on. Is not life more than food and the body more than clothing? Look at the birds of the air, for they neither sow nor reap nor gather into barns; yet your heavenly Father feeds them. Are you not of more value than they? Which of you by worrying can add one cubit to his stature?"*
>
> –Matthew 6:25-27 NKJV

We even hear worldly platitudes comparing us to birds. Haven't you heard people say, "She eats like a bird"?

Birds live very simply; they do not have elaborate homes. Their homes accommodate just the number of occupants who live there. Have you ever seen an oversized bird's nest? From Jesus' same lesson, but in a different book of the Bible, it says:

> *And he said unto them, "Take heed, and beware of covetousness: for a man's life consisteth not in the abundance of the things which he possesseth."*
> –Luke 12:15

You don't see birds trying to be something else. They are just birds that do what birds do. Birds rise up above situations; they fly high, like the eagle does. The worldly saying is "a bird's-eye view," which is a view from a very high place that allows you to see a large area (a greater perspective).

> *From the end of the earth will I cry unto thee, when my heart is overwhelmed: lead me to the rock that is higher than I.*
> –Psalm 61:2

In conclusion, this is what we learn from birds:

1. Rise up early and worship the Lord.
2. Eat simply; don't worry about what you will eat. God will make sure you are fed.
3. Dress simply. Don't worry about what you will wear.
4. Build simply and live in a place that is not beyond your means; do not covet and try to build even bigger houses.

5. Don't worry. When/if you do, look up, look up to the Lord; take yourself up above the situation. Fly high above it so you can see it from a greater perspective.
6. Be who you are—who God created you to be. Don't try to be someone else. Trust that God created you to be who you are.

Takeaway Nugget: Why not take a bird's-eye view of life?

Foundational Scripture: Look at the birds of the air, for they neither sow nor reap nor gather into barns; yet your heavenly Father feeds them. Are you not of *more* value than they?
–Matthew 6:26 NKJV

Week 2

Comes Highly Recommended

Name: Dr. Rapha. His first name is Jehovah. He has several locations, including offices right in your local area. His contact information is below:

Mobile: Is 53:5, Ps 107:20
Address: He's located on The Way between cross streets Truth and Life
Email: jrapha@yourhealer.com

Dr. Rapha does have an associate, Dr. Luke, who you can also see and is also an excellent physician.

Extremely flexible office hours, including 24-hour access.
Accepting new patients daily.
Insurances accepted:

- Accepts Blue Cross, prefers Calvary's Cross
- Accepts United Healthcare, prefers Unity of the Spirit Care
- Accepts Medicare, prefers ICare4U
- And a whole host of others!
- If you don't have insurance, that's okay, too. Just come as you are; He'll treat you without it.

Dr. Rapha's up on all the latest technology; however, He uses a lot of proven, tried-and-true remedies from centuries past.

Comes highly recommended. Excellent references are listed below:

- The woman with the issue of blood. She can be reached at the following address: Matthew 9:20-22, or on her cell phone at Luke 8:43-48
- Ten Lepers, but only one is reliable because he's the only one who maintained that healing by being thankful and following the doctor's instructions. (Luke 17:11-19)
- Jairus. (Mark 5:22-24)
- Mary and Martha (their last name is unknown; they are sisters of Lazarus). Cell phone: John 11:19-28; 39-40
- Bartimaeus can be reached at Mark 10:46-52.
- High-ranking official and former service man who was actually a Roman centurion. He can be reached at Matthew 8:5-13 and Luke 7:2-10.

I have used Dr. Rapha before and found Him to be competent, wise, patient, caring, and thorough. He's a little bit radical in His treatments, but one thing I do know is that He healed me! Give Him a call!

Takeaway Nugget: All healing comes from God!

Foundational Scripture: *For I will restore health unto thee, and I will heal thee of thy wounds, saith the LORD;*
–Jeremiah 30:17a

Week 3

Please Listen Carefully, as Our Menu Options Have Changed

Picture this: You are at a customer support center. Your number Psalm 139:1-3 has just been called.

> *"O LORD, You have searched me and known me. You know my sitting down and my rising up; You understand my thought afar off. You comprehend my path and my lying down, And are acquainted with all my ways."* (NKJV)

You are greeted by the rep at the counter.

Rep: My name is Holy Spirit, and I will be your Helper. How can I help you today?

You: I am here to upgrade my Christian walk.

Rep: Okay, great; I definitely can help you with that. We have a number of packages:

#1 - Confession and Repentance Package

With this one, you only need to bring in your existing stony heart, and we will give you an upgraded, new, regenerated heart. You can return your old one to any of our authentic church facilities. There are head shepherds at each location to help you with that exchange. And with this package, we are running a special: if you bring a friend, we'll give you two new hearts: one for you and one for your friend. This exchange is called repentance. It means "the act of changing one's mind." It is a complete turnaround from your old ways to embracing the will of God. See Matthew 9:13b.

You: Okay, that sounds good. How much is that package?

Rep: Oh, there is no charge. Just bring in your confession certificate signed by Jesus Christ. As long as His name is on it, you will be all set. With this package, you also get free deliverance.

#2 - Prayer Closet Refreshment Package

We will send a specialized design rep to your home to set up a room into which you can retreat.

> *But you, when you pray, go into your room, and when you have shut your door, pray to your Father who is in the secret place; and your Father who sees in secret will reward you openly.*
>
> –Matthew 6:6 (NKJV)

We'll install a surround-sound system so you can play praise and worship music. There will be a security lock that requires your personal access code to keep out kids, spouses, and everyone else. Only you have access to this room. A special ministry-of-artistry rep will decorate the room attractively and beautifully so that the atmosphere is set for you to have a special encounter with the Lord. As often as you go in there, you will receive. In there, you will receive peace, wisdom, instruction, purpose, correction, refreshment, insight, acceptance, healing and much more.

> *Come unto me, all ye that labor and are heavy laden, and I will give you rest.*
> –Matthew 11:28

#3 - Premium Package: The Strong Deliverance Package

This is a custom package tailored just for you. You will be assigned one of our highly trained reps to guide you through this process. There is a cost for this package, but it is well worth it. The fee for this package is your old habits, stubborn opposition, the desire to be free from strongholds, and the willingness to do something different. With this package, you will need to complete specialized modules:

- Fasting
- True brokenness, confession and repentance (the kind in Psalm 51)
- Extended prayer-time
- Raw transparency

Some of the side effects of this package are deep sobbing and wailing, crying out, vomiting, chills, birthing pains and other growing pains. These are temporary symptoms that will pass within a few days.

You will be assigned a mentor to help you with the process. There is a 24-hour hotline at 1-800-JESUSHELP in case you need after-hours support.

To sign up for this package, you will need to visit one of our authentic church facilities, but operators are standing by.

What I have written here is fun and lighthearted, but the message is true: Jesus is standing at the door of your heart, knocking. He wants you; He wants your heart. He wants to care for and love you all the days of your life! Repent and ask Him into your heart today. If you truly believe in your heart that you are a sinner and that God raised Jesus from the dead for your sins, then read the message below and on the next page and pray the prayer of salvation at the end.

During these end times - a day of reckoning - Jesus Christ is calling for all souls to be saved from the power of sin and death and to come to know Him and all He has done for us!

God made His gospel message, "the good news," simple, easy, practical and clear to be presented to anyone and everyone - common, ordinary people.

The only criteria needed to belong to Jesus is a desire to be set free, to be truly loved and cared for and to know the Truth that frees you; a love that doesn't box you in, or need to prove who you are; or to be accepted by mankind or need to pass man's qualifications. No stress, no yokes, no burdens. Just breathe, lie back and accept His peace, His power and His rest. (Tyler, Lois. The Reconciled Church, 2017)

> Heavenly Father, I come to You, acknowledging that I am a sinner in need of Your forgiveness. I believe that Jesus Christ died on the cross for my sins and that He rose again. I confess Jesus as my Lord and Savior; I invite Him into my heart to reign and rule over my life. Thank You for Your love, grace and forgiveness. In Jesus' name, I pray. Amen.

If you prayed the prayer sincerely from your heart, congratulations! You are saved! You have asked Jesus into your heart, and He immediately changed your heart and has accepted you. But now you must be discipled in the faith. You must learn and grow in your salvation. It's not enough just to pray that prayer and continue with your old life. You have been translated into a new life and you must come into the fullness of that new life. To do that, you must be taught. Tell a mature Christian that you have prayed this prayer and ask them to help you continue the process by finding a Bible-believing, Holy Spirit-led Christian church that believes in all three persons of the Trinity: Father, Son (Jesus) and the Holy Spirit. Welcome!

Takeaway Nugget: God wants a relationship with you!

Foundational Scripture: *For whosoever shall call upon the name of the Lord shall be saved.*
–Romans 10:13

Week 4

What's Your Crutch?

When I went in for counsel with my pastor, she said to me, "God will allow a crutch to stay in place for only so long before He removes it."

One January, my boss just up and announced she was leaving. I was very close to my boss; she was a great supervisor, support and friend to me. I was heartbroken, shaken and worried. I relied on her so much that I didn't know what I would do without her. It was a painful loss; I grieved for a few weeks. Soon after her departure, with the help of the Holy Spirit, I experienced great successes at work, and even more in the weeks that followed. I faced work challenges—some new, but many the same. I never would have thought or believed I could handle them so well. I leaned more on the Holy Spirit and He helped me with everything I needed.

Had my crutch not been removed, I never would have seen or known just how capable God's Spirit has made me. I would not have experienced what He will and can do through me when I cry out to Him and ask for His help. You can't know what God has put in you until a crutch has been removed.

Now read these words of Scripture:

> *After this there was a feast of the Jews; and Jesus went up to Jerusalem. Now there is at Jerusalem by the sheep market a pool, which is called in the Hebrew tongue Bethesda, having five porches.*

In these lay a great multitude of impotent folk, of blind, halt, withered, waiting for the moving of the water. For an angel went down at a certain season into the pool, and troubled the water: whosoever then first after the troubling of the water stepped in was made whole of whatsoever disease he had. And a certain man was there, which had an infirmity thirty and eight years. When Jesus saw him lie, and knew that he had been now a long time in that case, he saith unto him, Wilt thou be made whole? The impotent man answered him, Sir, I have no man, when the water is troubled, to put me into the pool: but while I am coming, another steppeth down before me. Jesus saith unto him, Rise, take up thy bed, and walk. And immediately the man was made whole, and took up his bed, and walked: and on the same day was the sabbath.
–John 5:1-9

After reading this passage, the Lord revealed to me that this man's excuses were his crutch. Those excuses allowed him to stay in a place where he didn't have to do anything. I believe that when Jesus asked him, "Do you want to be made well?" He was literally asking, "Do you want me to remove your crutch?" to which the man would have said no. Basically, Jesus was saying, "I'm going to remove your crutch; you just need to trust Me (Rise, take up your bed and walk). Get up from there, stop being afraid, get moving, and see what we can do together; see what I can do through you. Get up and start moving and living in your purpose. You'll then see what I put in you and what I created you to do."

And immediately the man was made well, took up his bed, and walked.
–John 5:9

"Walked" signifies that he got up and began to do what he was created to do, or at least that he was on his way.

So, the Lord asks you today: *What is your crutch*?

Is it:

- Anger, bitterness, unforgiveness - which prevent you from loving others and moving on.
- Fear - which prevents you from taking Spirit-led risks, from discovering what you're made of, what your gifts are, from stepping out and moving in what God is calling you to do. The fear crutch whispers, "I can't do that," "What if I fail?" "I don't know how" or "What will people say?"
- Depression - which allows you to feel sorry for yourself and causes you to hide, to stay under the radar, to go unnoticed and to never rise up.
- Jealousy or ingratitude - which keeps you focused on others—what they have and what their gifts are; never being satisfied with what God has given you or given you to do. It also keeps your heart hardened so that love cannot get through because your heart is blocked like a fortified city (nothing can get in; nothing can get out).
- Rejection - which keeps you from believing that you can ever accomplish anything. It never allows you to see what God can do in you. It keeps you

looking at yourself, keeps your focus looking inward and, if you're not careful, it can cross over into idolatry because you're always looking at yourself and how "bad" you are, which is not how God created you. Rejection keeps you listening to the lies of the enemy and others, and you'll never look to the One who is greater in you than he who is in the world.

- Dissatisfaction or disappointment - which keeps you grumbling, complaining and being negative. It never allows you to experience moments of joy because you can't see the positive in anything, which also makes you unpleasant to be around, so people avoid you.
- Criticism or judgment, whose root is the spirit of haughtiness (manifesting as arrogance and pride) - which keeps you always thinking more highly of yourself and entangles you in a web of legalism and perfectionism. It keeps you tied in knots because you have to continually prove that you're better than everyone else, which is exhausting. It's really related to the spirit of haughtiness and a deflection to keep you from acknowledging that you have character flaws and weaknesses of your own. Therefore, you don't forgive yourself and cannot experience God's grace, mercy and love.
- Worldly distractions/pleasures (TV, Internet, sports, shopping, food, sex or other indulgences) that keep you feeling unfulfilled. Your soul suffers lack. You can't experience abundant life or regeneration because you're not denying the flesh, not in the Word, not pursuing spiritual things and

not abiding in Christ so that you can truly press into Him.

The list goes on, but they all share this in common: they all have a payoff in your life and only you know what that payoff is. These things keep you stuck in the same place, like the man by the pool who said, "I have no man to put me into the pool when the water is stirred up." You're blocked from ever seeing who God really is—His character, His greatness, His magnificence, His power, His wisdom, His way of doing things, His might, His strength, His plan, His purpose for your life, His prosperity and His love.

That crutch is the easy way out. It requires no effort on your part, no creativity, no struggle, no processing, no deliverance, never having to think or figure it out. As long as you hold on to that crutch, you'll miss out on the journey and will never experience the kingdom of God, which is righteousness, peace and joy in the Holy Ghost. You'll never know the third person of the Trinity, the Helper in the person of the Holy Spirit, and you'll never enjoy any sense of awe and wonder about just who God is. You'll never realize His glory in your life.

God wants to be glorified through you and your life. So, today, Jesus says to you, right now, put down your crutch and "Rise, take up your bed and walk!"

Takeaway Nugget: Stop making excuses. Acknowledge your weaknesses and character flaws. Ask for the Holy Spirit's help. Get up, throw down your crutch, and walk!

Foundational Scripture: *For I know the plans I have for you, declares the LORD, plans to prosper you and not to harm you, to give you a future and a hope.*
–Jeremiah 29:11 (NIV)

Week 5

Have You Made Your Reservation?

> *The LORD is my shepherd; I shall not want. He maketh me to lie down in green pastures: he leadeth me beside the still waters. He restoreth my soul: he leadeth me in the paths of righteousness for his name's sake. Yea, though I walk through the valley of the shadow of death, I will fear no evil: for thou art with me; thy rod and thy staff they comfort me. Thou preparest a table before me in the presence of mine enemies: Thou anointest my head with oil; my cup runneth over. Surely goodness and mercy shall follow me all the days of my life: And I will dwell in the house of the LORD forever.*
>
> –Psalm 23:1-6

When I read that last line, I was encouraged and energized.

"I have a reservation in heaven!" I said out loud.

I have a reservation in heaven because I called ahead. I asked for a specific time (a predestined, appointed time) and stated how many would be in my party (those I'm bringing with me—family, friends, all I have witnessed to, those who accepted, and those who have yet to get on board).

Have you made yours?

If you don't have a reservation already made on the day you must give an account for your life, you are not guaranteed a seat (entrance). You may be denied and turned away by the Maître D or the Host. The restaurant I'm talking about is a classy establishment—one so classy that you cannot bribe your way in for a seat. The Maître D is too conventional to allow that. However, knowing Him personally (intimately) is a plus because He is so gracious and kind that He does not want to turn anyone away. Now, because this is fine dining, if you've called ahead, your reservation is secure and you have no need to worry that it's not. You don't have to keep checking back. Rest assured, you'll get in.

Also, it's very important to remember that if you don't make a reservation, it's likely that they may be completely booked and you may find yourself completely shut out and unable to dine. You'll be out in the cold—well, actually in the heat, as the case may be.

> *And while they went to buy, the bridegroom came; and they that were ready went in with him to the marriage: and the door was shut.*
> –Matthew 25:10

Making a reservation is easy; you can call at any time (prayer of salvation). Even if you don't reach the Maître D directly, you can always leave a message. He will hear you!

> *For whosoever shall call upon the name of the Lord shall be saved.*
> –Romans 10:13

Now, you may include several people in your party, as many as you like, actually; however, in order for them to be seated with you, the Maître D must also have their names written in His lambskin appointment book. Each must have called and established their own reservation with Him. They must know Him personally and intimately, just as you do.

> *And whosoever was not found written in the book of life was cast into the lake of fire.*
> –Revelation 20:15

Now, once you have made your reservation and know that it's secure, you need to read the menu and become very familiar with it. That way, when you arrive at the dining establishment, you'll know what to order, how everything works and that you're in the right place. The menu is quite extensive; many find that it's actually a book! Depending on the appointed time of your reservation, it may be a long time before you get to the place. If you delve into the menu and feast your eyes on it, you won't experience that last-minute indecision of what to dine on. Many people wait and then, when faced with all those extensive choices, they find themselves flustered about what to order. Reading the menu beforehand will give you peace.

Now, be aware: There are counterfeit restaurants that claim to have the same type of menu, but you must be discerning about those places, as their food is not the same quality. Their food isn't prepared with the best ingredients and, in many cases, is watered down. Another thing about those other dining establishments is that they're very hot inside. The heat is always turned way up, even in the summer. There are many people dining at those places, enjoying the food, not realizing they are at the wrong restaurant.

> *And many false prophets shall rise, and shall deceive many.*
> –Matthew 24:11

If you are saved, dwelling in God's house forever is His promise to you; however, you must make your reservation and then keep it by showing up. But what you do between the time of your reservation and that great meal is key. While you are waiting, you must sup from the menu often and live your life as an overcomer.

> *To him that overcometh will I grant to sit with me in my throne, even as I also overcame, and am set down with my Father in his throne.*
> –Revelation 3:21

> *He that overcometh shall inherit all things; and I will be his God, and he shall be my son.*
> –Revelation 21:7

If you have done that, then you can have the assurance of eternal life, dwelling in the house of the Lord forever.

Takeaway Nugget: Jesus is the only bridge and the only way to eternal life. Without a relationship with Him, you will be eternally separated from God.

Foundational Scripture: *For God so loved the world, that he gave his only begotten Son, that whosoever believeth in him should not perish, but have everlasting life.*
–John 3:16

Week 6

Keep Your Focus to Stay in Your Lane

In my city, there is a weird four-lane road. The two left lanes are for left turns, and the two right lanes are for going straight ahead. There are two green arrows for the left-turn lanes. At any given time, two of the lights are cycling between red/stop and green/left arrows, and the other two are cycling between regular red and green lights. So, the two left-turn lanes might be red while the two straight-ahead lanes might be green.

This is a road I took to work every day. One morning, my left-turn arrows turned green while the other two were red, but just as I was about to turn, they flashed green. For a split second, I was confused—not for long, but just long enough to make me notice.

"Audrey, keep your focus!" I said out loud to myself. At that moment, God ministered this to me: we must keep our focus to stay in our lane. Keep your eyes on Jesus and do not look at the other signals or lanes. Something completely different is going on in those lanes that has nothing to do with you.

> *Let thine eyes look right on, and let thine eyelids look straight before thee.*
>
> –Proverbs 4:25

Later, He ministered this; read this through a spiritual lens. Suppose you had not been paying attention to your lane and had veered into the lane to your right (the straight-ahead lane), causing an accident. Here are the consequences. First, you have hit another driver and, because you were not focused, you have disrupted another person's plans. You have caused that person to stumble. Also, you have damaged their car. Their vehicle now has nicks and bumps that weren't there before. Therefore, you have caused wounds and scars that will take time to be repaired. It may take some time now for that person to heal.

Second, let's say your car is totaled. Now you have to start all over from the beginning. The Lord has to take you back, despite the progress you have made—or thought you had made, because your eyes wandered into a lane that had nothing to do with you. This was a lane not designed for you to be in. There is now a cost associated with this mishap—in this case, an unexpected financial burden. Now you really must lean on Him, in faith, to help you come up with the funds to cover the damages. This may require you to make sacrifices you had not planned for. It may also require you to humble yourself and ask God to help you examine why you were so distracted with focusing on another lane. Seek the Lord for the reason your focus is off.

Another far-reaching consequence is that, because of your accident in the straight-ahead lanes, all the traffic behind you is now blocked. They are stuck and unable to move forward. Your lack of focus has now held up others from getting to where they were trying to go. You have caused a delay in the lives of countless people, all for whom God also has a purpose. Their plans are now altered and put on hold until the mess you made is cleared.

Now, the Lord understands that you did not do this on purpose, and He will come to your aid. He is your Helper, but nonetheless, there are still consequences associated with your actions. Now, think of all those souls who are hanging in the balance—lives that are on hold because they're waiting on your obedience. To be sure, God's purpose for their lives will be accomplished, but there will be a delay for them as He now has to start over with you and for them.

What has God purposed for you to do? How are you seeking Him for that purpose? Are you learning to be content with the life and purpose He has for you? If there is something in your lane you don't like, ask God about it. There is a purpose for it and maybe He has to change you so that you will see the beauty and value in the purpose He ordained for you.

Get to know Him intimately, and you will come to see who you really are. Your purpose will become clearer and clearer.

> *Delight thyself also in the LORD: And he shall give thee the desires of thine heart.*
> —Psalm 37:4

You don't know the true desires of your heart until you know the Creator. Only He knows the purpose for which He designed you, and to know that, you must get to know Him. That's the only way you'll be able to keep your focus so that you can stay in your lane.

> *You know me inside and out, you know every bone in my body; You know exactly how I was*

made, bit by bit, how I was sculpted from nothing into something. Like an open book, you watched me grow from conception to birth; all the stages of my life were spread out before you, The days of my life all prepared before I'd even lived one day.

—Psalm 139:15-16 (The Message)

Keep your focus and stay in your lane!

Takeaway Nugget: Even before birth, God has given every person unique gifts and talents to make a difference in this world. Yes, even you. Only you can use them through Him, the way He desires.

Foundational Scripture: ...*But each one has his own gift from God, one in this manner and another in that.*

—1 Corinthians 7:7b (NKJV)

Week 7

The Greatest Super Bowl Showdown Ever

The Super Bowl is usually held on the first Sunday in February. People gear up for it like it's a national holiday, and I believe this next one is going to be the greatest Super Bowl showdown or matchup ever in history!

The two teams are in fierce opposition to one another, each seeking to win over fans to their side. Even people who are not all that interested in the Super Bowl tend to be drawn to one team or the other for various reasons, including mundane ones like favoring one team's colors better.

Since I don't follow football at all, I had to ask which teams are in the league this year. I was told that the matchup is between:

THE WORLD VS. THE KINGDOM OF GOD

Lately, I, my pastor, my church and many others in the body of Christ, have all been very grieved about the plight of the youth and their souls. For me, it's particularly the young women who have my heart. Fortunately, many others have the young men covered! We are losing our youth. As news of those even in our midst who are pulling away from the things of God comes to the forefront, I am saddened and grieved about what will become of them, certainly eternally, and also right here, right now, as they struggle with the pressures of the world.

Because this has been on my heart, I began meditating on it and talking it over with the Lord so I can understand. I asked Him why. The obvious answer is that the world has more of a pull on them than the church. Then, I began to meditate on why that is. What does the world have to offer them over the kingdom of God? Now, of course, as followers of Christ, we know better, but I began to lay it all out so I could see it plainly, in hopes that we will continue to pray effectual, fervent prayers and help them come to understand how empty the world is. Their spirit needs to be awakened so that the Holy Spirit can impart to them that the world has nothing to offer. Life in the kingdom of God far exceeds anything the world can offer!

The following chart compares what the world offers versus what the kingdom of God offers.

The World	The Kingdom of God
Sleepless nights, tossing and turning, wide awake, worrying about problems that always seem worse in the dark of night. Groping for sleep aids that leave you groggy or even worse: do not work at all.	Deep, peaceful, restful sleep that sustains you through the entire night until the alarm goes off or the Lord wakes you up (which He does, whether the alarm goes off or not)! *I will both lie down in peace, and sleep; For You alone, O LORD, make me dwell in safety.*

The World	The Kingdom of God
	–Psalm 4:8 (NKJV) Oftentimes, He will awaken you before the alarm sounds so you can read, pray, or spend quiet time with Him.
Problems that you cannot solve, endless worrying, and inability to make decisions because you just don't know what to do.	Wisdom from above; true wisdom, where God will tell you how to pray beforehand, show you where to go, open the right doors, and/or will create circumstances that allow you to meet with the right people at the right time, in the right place. Only God can do that! *Trust in the LORD with all thine heart; and lean not unto thine own understanding. In all thy ways acknowledge him, and he shall direct thy paths.* –Proverbs 3:5-6
Difficulties at work or just in life in general, because you do not understand aspects of your job, or you are faced with a task that	God will show you how to do it!

The World	The Kingdom of God
you don't quite know how to do.	He will. He will open up your understanding to show you just what to do. I once needed help with a math calculation on income averages that I just did not understand. I prayed to God to help me, declaring first that "I have the mind of Christ," and that no one knows how to help me with a math problem better than Jesus, the Creator of the universe and the One who invented math. I just prayed for Jesus to help me understand it. It took a little while as I sat in a conference room alone, poring over the charts. Finally, I got upset and moped to the Lord, "I thought you said you would help me with this." He heard my pitiful cry. After praying and reading it again, I understood! It was as *clear* as it could be. God is amazing! And then the Lord spoke this to me

The World	The Kingdom of God
	through a co-worker; it was a journal message that said, "Everything you need is already inside of you, and when you go to God to ask for His help, He just pulls up what He's already deposited in you." I did a happy dance right there on that one! You can, too! My pastor often speaks about tasks that God has given her to do, for which she has had no training or education. However, God supernaturally shows her how to do it by the power of the Holy Spirit! The Holy Spirit will show us just what to do. *But the Comforter, which is the Holy Ghost, whom the Father will send in my name, he shall teach you all things, and bring all things to your remembrance, whatsoever I have said unto you.* –John 14:26

The World	The Kingdom of God
	I can do all things through Christ, which strengtheneth me. —Philippians 4:13
Gaping emptiness, loneliness, a void, a hole that can't be filled, deep longing for love, fulfillment, and satisfaction that leads to meaningless, empty, momentary sexual pleasure, appetite issues, addictions, and cravings that can never be fulfilled.	Guidance, fulfillment, vision, direction, and a meaningful, impactful purpose that will bless countless others. It's the kingdom principle that when you are walking in purpose, God will be glorified, the people will be edified, and you will be sanctified! The hole is filled up with God's love, security, safety, sense of belonging, and a shalom peace that truly surpasses your understanding. It's His love—His deep abiding love in the form of *intimacy*! (Never leaving you nor forsaking you). It's the assurance of belonging that the world cannot take away. *Peace I leave with you, my peace I give unto you: not as the world giveth, give I unto*

The World	The Kingdom of God
	you. Let not your heart be troubled, neither let it be afraid. –John 14:27
Loneliness, lack of companionship, and genuine connection; no friends. "I don't have any friends, and the ones I do have are lame."	Fellowship with like-minded believers who will support you as you could never have imagined. People who will be there for you no matter what. People who see you and have seen you at your very worst, but do not bat an eyelash because they understand, and all they want to do is help you and stand with you as you go through your trials. People who love you as unconditionally as humans are able to do. They are a comforting, safe place to run into. And far greater than that is Jesus, who is a friend like no other. He's there 24/7. He won't hang up on you; He'll listen without interrupting and will undergird and sustain you when you are at your

The World	The Kingdom of God
	worst. He is someone who already understands you; unlike human beings who wrinkle their brows as you speak, because you know what you want to say, yet they totally misunderstand you. God understands; you don't have to interpret it for Him. *"A man who has friends must himself be friendly, but there is a friend who sticks closer than a brother."* –Proverbs 18:24 (NKJV)
Financial difficulties, worrying about financial difficulties, and trouble making ends meet.	Endless resources through tithes and offerings. When you commit to giving the 10%, God will cover and sanctify the other 90% of your income, and He will provide supernatural creative financing for you. The numbers in your budget will just not add up! You will have a surplus, though your

The World	The Kingdom of God
	calculator shows you in the red! I am a living witness. There will be favor when losses occur; connections with the right people who will bless you and will say out loud, "I don't know why you're getting this credit or discount, but the system is showing a credit." Times when God will help you recoup a loss with an unexpected financial blessing. (Using an ATM, I once had $600 stolen from my credit union account. The *next* day, I received an unexpected $2000 bonus from my employer, and my credit union, against their policy, ended up giving me back $200 after I petitioned for them to show me grace. *For the LORD God is a sun and shield: the LORD will give grace and glory: No good thing will he withhold*

The World	The Kingdom of God
	from them that walk uprightly. –Psalm 84:11
Harsh words, unforgiving attitudes, mean-spirited people who will bring condemning words, heap on guilt, and who will try to demean you and speak negatively about you. People who reject you and who never support the purpose and plan that God has for your life.	Forgiveness through confession. The voice of a loving Father, saying, "It's okay, I forgive you. It's over; you've confessed with a sincere heart, and I accept and honor your confession. Now forget about it." *There is therefore now no condemnation to them which are in Christ Jesus, who walk not after the flesh, but after the Spirit.* –Romans 8:1 *For as the heaven is high above the earth, so great is his mercy toward them that fear him.* *As far as the east is from the west, so far hath he removed our transgressions from us.* –Psalm 103:11-12

The World	The Kingdom of God
	...wherein he hath made us accepted in the beloved. —Ephesians 1:6b
Darkness in everything around us—TV shows and other forms of entertainment; perverse, unholy, disturbing, spirit-invading, loud, vulgar music and images. Ghosts, zombies, vampires, satanic images. TV shows that promote and glorify greed, scandal, corruption, adultery, and murder. Titles around the time of this writing include: *Scandal, Betrayal, How to Get Away with Murder, Lie to Me*. And don't kid yourself: as you constantly put that stuff into your eye and ear gates, you take on that darkness as it slowly seeps in overtime as you consistently "fellowship" with that stuff. It's something to pray about in your prayer closet. As a new fall lineup begins,	In God's presence, there is sweetness, a wholesome, peaceful presence; joy, light, truth, love, holiness, purity, and a place of safety. A refuge and a place of escape. A calming, embracing, gentle place to rest. A place where you can truly hear His voice because the atmosphere is clean, fresh, light, airy, refreshing, and *holy*! *Thou wilt shew me the path of life: in thy presence is fullness of joy; at thy right hand there are pleasures for evermore.* —Psalm 16:11

The World	The Kingdom of God
maybe it's time to make a decision about such shows and movies so that you can bring greater purpose to your life and glory to God.	
Sickness, disease, ailments with no basis, nagging pains, and conditions with no diagnosis. Taking medications that cannot cure you; if they did, you wouldn't need to keep taking them!	Health (not "good health;" you're either in health or you're not). Wellness, well-being; freedom from ailments, conditions, and pains that have no basis. Healed and completely cured with no recurrence. Someone who can truly get to the root of the problem, reveal it to you, and then do the work in you *for you* to fix and heal the problem! Who else does that? Who else *can* do that? Nobody but *Jesus*! *Beloved, I wish above all things that thou mayest prosper and be in health, even as thy soul prospereth.* –3 John 1:2

The world has nothing to offer.

For what shall it profit a man, if he shall gain the whole world, and lose his own soul?
–Mark 8:36

How can we show youth and others the kingdom of God and all it has to offer? We must pray and talk with them. More importantly than that, we must model godly behavior before them to choose the ways of life; to choose righteousness over things of the world. My pastor says, "More is caught than taught."

I call heaven and earth as witnesses today against you, that I have set before you life and death, blessing and cursing; therefore choose life, that both you and your descendants may live;
–Deuteronomy 30:19 NKJV

For which team are you rooting? Which team has more of a pull on you? The "Kingdom of God's" righteous team or "The World's" team? And don't be deceived; you may be more on the side of the world's team than you know.

Seek God and ask the Holy Spirit to reveal to you which side you're truly on. Also, ask yourself: how would I tell someone else what it looks like to be in the righteous kingdom of God? That is your testimony of how Jesus has changed your life and made it abundant. This is what you must share with the youth of this generation!

I am so glad that I am on Team Kingdom of God! I have been adopted into His family, His way of doing things, His favor, His protection, and His blessing. I am so glad that He knows me, desires me, loves me and wants me. It is a security I have never known, and for which there is no comparison. I want nothing to do with the world, its ways, its irreverence, its darkness and its harshness. We must tell our young people that the world has nothing to offer them. There is nothing in it or of it that will satisfy the deep longing of their souls. We must show them, tell them and pray for them so that they'll wake up to the enemy's deceptive lies. We must pray down the strongholds that keep them in bondage to fear.

I am blessed and feel blessed to know that there is always a place of love, of kindness, of favor, of honor, of integrity, of guidance, of health, of strength, of help, of understanding of who I am and what I'm dealing with; of mercy, of grace, of forgiveness, of joy, of companionship, of intimacy, of safety, of connectedness, of prosperity, of comfort, of purpose, of direction, of wisdom, of protection, of soul satisfaction, of cleanliness, of revelation, of truth and of life. And that place is only in Jesus, with Jesus, of Jesus, by Jesus and for Jesus! Touchdown!

Takeaway Nugget: Your opponent has already been defeated at the cross of Jesus!

Foundational Scripture: *Thus saith the LORD unto you, Be not afraid nor dismayed by reason of this great multitude; for the battle is not yours, but God's.*
–2 Chronicles 20:15b

Week 8

A 5-Day Practical Guide For "Behaving Like a Christian"

Whenever God moves us or elevates us, there ought to be something different—an overall change in our character. Old things, old habits, old thoughts, old attitudes and certainly old behaviors ought to be left behind. He doesn't move us for us to stay the same. He has a plan and it's up to us to move forward with it.

> *"Brethren, I do not count myself to have apprehended; but one thing I do, forgetting those things which are behind and reaching forward to those things which are ahead, I press toward the goal for the prize of the upward call of God in Christ Jesus.*
>
> –Philippians 3:13-14 (NKJV)

One way we can do this is to really focus on the commandments God gave us in His word. We ought to put them into practice.

The following is a 5-Day Guide to help us practice what we preach, as it were. One of the words to start with is focus. Let's focus each day this week on a specific command from God's Word. Let's practice the following commands this week.

Day 1: Gratitude/Thanksgiving

Verse: *In everything give thanks...* (1 Thessalonians 5:18a)

Assignment: Be thankful today! Start the day by thanking God. Throughout the entire day, thank God for everything you see, encounter and experience. We are not asked to thank God for every situation, but to be thankful in every situation because we know Him and that He is in control. Even in challenging circumstances or times of illness, we can thank God. We can seek the Holy Spirit and then give thanks from His perspective. Whether in good times or in bad times, we can give thanks! Thank God throughout this day for His goodness!

Day 2: Idle Words

Verse: *But I say unto you, That every idle word that men shall speak, they shall give account thereof in the day of judgment.* (Matthew 12:36)

Assignment: Tame your tongue! Watch what you say today. Be careful with the words you speak. Pay close attention to what is about to come out or what has already come out of your mouth. Think about your words. Is it necessary to say what you're about to say? Does it bring glory to God? Often, we speak out some foolish things that just aren't necessary. Are the words you're speaking going to hurt or offend someone? Be careful not to use sarcasm which is often couched in "Oh, I was just teasing." Do not gossip, which is sometimes hidden in, "Pray for so and so..." which can be a way of talking about their situation. Look up Scriptures on what our speech is supposed to be like, and be mindful of what you say all day.

Day 3: Think of Others

Verse: *Let each of you look out not only for his own interests, but also for the interests of others.* (Philippians 2:4 NKJV)

Assignment: A pastor once challenged her readers with this task: every time you start thinking of yourself—*stop*! Get your mind off yourself. Today, think of the interests of others. Practice being unselfish all day today. Even while driving, think of others in your life and pray for them today. Think of ways you can bless others today with a kind word, a smile or a gesture that lets them know that you put them first.

Day 4: Examine Yourself

Verse: *Examine me, O LORD, and prove me; try my reins and my heart.* (Psalm 26:2)

Assignment: Examine yourself today! Seek the Lord about your character, your thought life, your attitude and your behavior. Ask Him to reveal those things that are still deeply hidden—things that are keeping you from His plan for your life. Things that are holding you back, even in natural things. Ask Him to reveal those strongholds, those things that are deeply rooted that do not want to let go of you. Be truthful with yourself today. Let what is revealed bring you to a place of repentance and godly sorrow. Cry, cry out and pray in desperation for the Holy Spirit to help you overcome. Listen to what God is saying and do not try to excuse it away! He already knows what you're like; He wants to help you overcome!

Day 5: Forgive

Verse: *For if ye forgive men their trespasses, your heavenly Father will also forgive you: But if ye forgive not men their trespasses, neither will your Father forgive your trespasses.* (Matthew 6:14-15)

Assignment: Forgive! Forgive freely. Forgiveness is a choice; it is an action. You can choose to forgive. Practice having a forgiving heart today, even in those small offenses that come your way: traffic mishaps, a cashier's unfriendliness, etc. Choose to forgive. Choose to let it go and pray for the person. Seek God about those people in your life that He wants you to forgive. If you already know who they are, forgive them. State out loud to Him,

"I choose to forgive <fill in the person's name> for <fill in the specific offense>."

Be specific about the perceived or real offense you endured and then forgive. Say to the Holy Spirit, "Now, help my emotions come in line with the words I have just spoken. Work this forgiveness in my heart." Give it a try. Your flesh won't like it, but your obedience will be rewarded. You will begin to be set free from the prison of unforgiveness.

After the five days, review each day to see how you did. Let God speak to you in areas where you could have done better. Continue to read the Word and cry out to Him for deliverance. Remember all that Jesus sacrificed on the cross to make you an overcomer!

Takeaway Nugget: To see results, you must practice the disciplines.

Foundational Scripture: *But be ye doers of the word, and not hearers only, deceiving your own selves.*
−James 1:22

Week 9

Exposed

Exposed: make something visible, typically by uncovering it.

Synonyms for *exposed*: bare, naked, disclosed, uncovered, unprotected, clear, divulged, exhibited, revealed, open, shown, unmasked, stripped, unveiled, apparent, brought to light, dug up, found out, laid bare, made manifest, on display, on the spot, unconcealed, unhidden, visible.

Why are we so afraid to expose ourselves? What is it that we are so afraid of if someone knows something about us that we think makes us look vulnerable or weak?

The following came from a prayer I was praying for someone struggling with addiction. It said that the addiction to "whatever it is" is only a symptom of the real root: hurt, rejection, bitterness, resentment, unhealed wounds, and a lack of esteem and love for oneself. The prayer called for the person praying it to seek God to expose the sins of unforgiveness, bitterness, judgment of others, evil speaking, hatred of others or self, wrath, sinful anger or jealousy.

What is so terrifying about saying how we really feel, what our childhood was like, or our current condition? What if we just took the plunge and said:

"My father never told me he loved me."

"My mother called me stupid repeatedly."

"I am a slob."

"I need you."

"I grew up in a home of strife, yelling and bickering."

"My father committed suicide, and I am angry with him for leaving me."

"I am depressed."

"I am asking you to hear my heart."

"My mother was an alcoholic and a mean one at that."

"I just want you to tell me I am a good husband."

"I never received hugs growing up."

"I love you."

"No one ever said they were proud of me."

"I feel ugly."

"I am afraid of dying."

"I just want to spend time with you."

"I am afraid to fail."

"I can't stop gambling."

"I was sexually abused."

"I don't like it when you're mean to me."

"I know I've not been the best father to you."

"I never learned how to keep house."

"I am jealous of my brother."

"I want to tell you that I was wrong and I apologize."

"I want you to tell me I am beautiful."

"I miss you when you're away."

There. We said it. We expressed something deep inside. What happened? The world didn't stop. We didn't die. The people whose opinions we cared about may have been shocked for a moment. They may not have known what to say, or what was said may have made them pause just long enough to actually consider what you said, opening up a conversation. Just a simple expression of what's on your heart could spark a whole new depth in a relationship that has been stagnant or even hostile.

Sometimes, we just need to express what's inside. Sometimes, we just need to hear others or they need to hear us. The people in our lives who truly do not have our best interests at heart may try to take what you said and use it against you or may even ridicule you. They may try to brush it off or minimize what you just voiced out. However, being in relationship with the one true living God assures you that He will be your defender and will not allow a formed weapon to prosper against you. Yes, it may form, but it will not prosper.

Oftentimes, what they say or do reveals the hurting condition of their heart and has nothing to do with you. You can take their backlash to your prayer closet. It may take a minute for you to get there, but you can ask God to build character in you by asking Him to help you forgive them, to pray for their salvation and to release them from their own bondage. Some of them may react very negatively to the truth you just spoke out and then hold a grudge; again, that has nothing to do with you. Remember this: light exposes darkness. Darkness doesn't like light; it can't even understand it. The Bible says,

> *And the light shineth in darkness; and the darkness comprehended it not.*
>
> –John 1:5

Take their "darkness" to God and pray for them. Keep in mind that some of those people are so self-absorbed that they'll forget about you and what you said in about 10 minutes.

More importantly though, the people who are close to you and truly care about you will likely express sympathy or empathy for what you just shared. Most of them have felt or experienced something similar, and many of them will offer words of comfort. Most will even nod in acknowledgment. To your surprise, if they really do care about you, you might find them to be quite supportive and willing to share their own story, ultimately bringing you relief, knowing that you're not alone.

The enemy loves to convince you that you are "the only one." Exposing your feelings may cause you a moment of pain as you begin to remember and face the past. However, it can also bring great relief, as if a burden has been lifted. This is where the healing can now begin.

The enemy wants to keep you locked, blocked and tied up in knots where you have no peace and are forever tormented by those feelings of emptiness, loneliness, bitterness, discontent, and dissatisfaction, trapped in a vicious cycle of never feeling resolved, whole or well. Holding it in has now created a sense of pride and arrogance in you. As a result, you walk around trying to cover up what's really going on inside you. You now appear to others as someone no one really wants to be around. You've just accomplished the exact opposite of what you really want, which is to be accepted and loved.

Holding it all in is a major cause of physical symptoms, both diagnosed and undiagnosed, as well as general feelings of anxiety, stress and hopelessness. Worse yet, you are numb—a walking dead person at odds with those who want to be close to you. Your relationships are tense, and a false peace exists between you and those you interact with. Is living like this really worth it, when all you have to do is speak a few words out loud in a complete sentence? To tell the truth about how you really feel or the condition you're in?

Truth. Think about that word for a moment as you read this definition: being that which is the case rather than what is manifest or assumed. That definition speaks volumes. It says, "rather than what is manifest." That means you may think you're hiding and covering *it, but people often see through what you're not saying, especially those with spiritual discernment. Pain is difficult to hide. God is truth, and Psalm 51 says* that *He desires truth in the inward parts.*

Being open, honest, and truthful brings release, liberty, deliverance, and freedom. The Bible says,

> *And ye shall know the truth, and the truth shall make you free."*
>
> –John 8:32

God wants us to be honest, open, and truthful with others and with ourselves. Pray and ask the Holy Spirit which person you should share with, not just any person, but a trusted one. A simple expression of what's on your heart, spoken with the right person in God's timing—could open up what could be one of the best conversations you've ever had. When you trust God with your feelings and your state, He can do amazing things, far beyond all that you can ask or think.

> *"Now unto him that is able to do exceeding abundantly above all that we ask or think, according to the power that worketh in us."*
> –Ephesians 3:20

God is in control of the other person's heart; He's doing a work in them as well as in you. If you trust God, though it may be difficult or painful to say what's on your heart, you just never know what He can do as those words of truth fall on the other person's ears. God loves us and knows the hidden cries of our heart. When we cry out to Him in sincerity and trust Him, He will lead us to a place of healing, either by moving on the heart of the other person or by comforting us Himself if things don't immediately go the way we would have liked. Nonetheless, we must trust the Sovereign Lord of the universe, the One who created us. We must trust the One who is omniscient and who works all things together for good with whatever we express to another in truth, in purity, and in love. Stop being afraid to express the truth, and let Him handle the outcome.

Sometimes, such expressions of truth stir up or dredge up old wounds and pain that we don't just know how to handle. In those cases, there is nothing wrong with seeking godly, spiritual counseling or a deliverance ministry. A wise, mature, Holy Spirit-led pastor or counselor can guide you on a path to wellness, with Jesus as the ultimate Healer who brings about complete wholeness. Trust God with what you need to express to Him or another person and then just open your mouth and say it. God will take it from there if you pray and ask Him to do so.

Takeaway Nugget: Can we talk…?

Foundational Scripture: *Trust in the LORD with all thine heart; and lean not unto thine own understanding. In all thy ways acknowledge him, and he shall direct thy paths.*
–Proverbs 3:5, 6

Week 10

"Recalculating"

There is no doubt you have a GPS; if not, you probably have some navigation device on your cell phone to help you find a particular location. If you miss your turn or choose to go another way, the device will pause and then say, "Recalculating." The destination has not changed; the device was programmed to be kind enough to reroute you rather than leaving you lost without knowing where to go next.

If you are a person who is stubborn, controlling, legalistic, religious or just a creature of habit and routine, "recalculating" doesn't always compute. It's uncomfortable and unfamiliar. I have come to the revelation that the Christian life must be lived as one of "recalculating." We must be ready to adjust to changes and unexpected turns. That's what life is made of. Even the world has the saying, "The only thing that doesn't change in life is that things change." And certainly that's the true definition of a life that's laid down and totally surrendered to the will of God. We must always be ready to move, act, or go in a different direction as the Holy Spirit leads. Be ready. We never know what God is going to do, so we must always be poised and willing to be flexible when asked to do something different.

Recalculating means that you are willing to forgo a lifestyle of convenience and tradition. The Christian life is meant to be one of adventure, not the norm all the time. This life is refreshing, filled with newness and Holy

Spirit-led purpose. It's not a boring, mundane, humdrum life! It's meant to be full and abundant; how can it be if you are never willing to step out of your comfort zone and "recalculate"?

When you're not willing to recalculate, you risk missing out on so much that the Lord has in store for you. One day, I was driving somewhere, and for whatever reason, I couldn't take the route that was originally programmed. As the device recalculated, I ended up turning down streets I had never been down before. I saw an area of my city that was new to me. As I took it all in, I remember saying, "Oh, I didn't know this was back here." It was fascinating and eye-opening.

When you really think about it, "recalculating" is a life of trust and obedience. When you are willing to truly follow the Holy Spirit's prompts without knowing the plan or the agenda, He always leads you into new, uncharted territory that is more beautiful and fruitful than your normal, often stale routine. When you are willing to relax and go with the flow, your faith elevates. You grow stronger and hopefully wiser because you have seen and learned something new. You'll get stretched and see capabilities that you never knew existed. God knows, though, and He is trying to get you to come up higher in Him. God will never lead you astray.

Jesus is a good shepherd—the Good Shepherd who said,

> *"My sheep hear my voice, and I know them, and they follow me: And I give unto them eternal life; and they shall never perish, neither shall any man pluck them out of my hand. My Father, which gave them me, is greater than all; and no man is able to pluck them out of my Father's hand."*
>
> –John 10:27-29

So, practice "recalculating." It's not that difficult with the Holy Spirit's leading. Go a different way to work. Be safe and use wisdom, but try turning down streets you've never been down before. Shop at a mall that you have never been to before. Try a different menu item. Willingly accept a task you've never done. Say yes to an event that you've never considered attending. Engage in conversation with someone you haven't talked with before. Share a testimony with someone who needs to hear it. Open yourself to new possibilities. These are all ways of recalculating.

When things are not going the way I expect now, I am truly learning to say (sometimes out loud), "Uh oh, recalculating." So, live, breathe, and enjoy the life that God has purposed for you by learning to be more trusting, open and free. Let the Holy Spirit take you on the adventure of a lifetime!

Takeaway Nugget: Come out of the comfort zone!

Foundational Scripture: *The steps of a good man are ordered by the LORD: and he delighteth in his way.*
–Psalm 37:23

Week 11

Hurdles

Hurdling is the act of running and jumping over an obstacle at speed.

We are all in a race. We are assigned different lanes; however, our destination is the same for us all. We are at different levels of maturity in our training regimen, but God asks us to keep our eyes on the finish line and stay in our own lane. When we are running a race—and let's say it's our first marathon, we have to train. Spiritually, there are obstacles (hurdles) that are in our way. We must learn to jump *over* them.

"Obstacles" are those hurdles (the white bars)

Obstacles = emotions, patterns of thinking, and bad behaviors

These hurdles take the form of repeated patterns (tending to worry as soon as you have a symptom), reactions based on wounds of the past (feeling rejected and condemned at the first mention of correction, which you only see as criticism), and emotional eating to soothe your feelings of depression. These are just a few examples; there are countless others.

The enemy is trying to trip us up with these obstacles (he attacks us with the same weapons—the ones he knows we'll fall for). We open the door because we have rehearsed the same patterns over and over and continue to operate in them. And while the enemy is certainly not all-knowing, he studies our behavior patterns and habits.

When you are first learning how to jump the hurdles, you are going to knock them down a lot. But as you continue to train and practice (reading and studying the Word), you'll become more adept and stronger, and you won't knock down as many hurdles as before. Eventually, God enables you to jump over all of them.

> *Many are the afflictions of the righteous: but the LORD delivereth him out of them all.*
> –Psalm 34:19

Ask the Holy Spirit to help you identify your thought patterns, attitudes and reactions the minute something comes to trip you up. Good indicators that this is happening are: anger, depression, feelings of retaliation, unforgiving thoughts, bitterness, complaining, pride/haughtiness, anxiety, stress and physical symptoms.

When these "triggers" occur, ask the Holy Spirit to help you pinpoint the hurdle that the enemy has dredged up. Just know that when the enemy attacks us with these things, he doesn't realize that he is actually helping us by giving us an opportunity to be conformed to the image of God.

> *But the God of all grace, who hath called us unto his eternal glory by Christ Jesus, after that ye have suffered a while, make you perfect, stablish, strengthen, settle you.*
> –1 Peter 5:10

God will use obstacles and the enemy's roadblocks to help us overcome. And in the overcoming, we are being made stronger and can bring God more glory. This is why we cannot get stuck in being so upset with ourselves that we are not further along. We must realize that this is a process and God is using these "obstacles" to perfect us to make us better so that our faith will grow. That way, we will learn how to lean on and cry out to the Holy Spirit for help, so that we can cope and endure by using the tools He has given us. We will be equipped to work through these situations with kingdom principles.

When we use God's methods, His ways, His weapons, His strategies—in essence, all the teachings in His Word, we will overcome; no, we *do* overcome. And then, each time we face the same challenge or obstacle again, we will handle it so much better. It won't be as difficult as the last time, and we will eventually get to the place where we say, "Oh wow, I didn't react to that the way I used to." That's how we know that healing and growth have manifested. Satan will push the button, but we won't jump!

So, remember: when these challenges come up, just know that God is using them to perfect you. Cry out to Him and be comforted by His Word.

Takeaway Nugget: Even when I don't see it, You're working. Even when I don't feel it, You're working.

Foundational Scripture: *Being confident of this very thing, that He who has begun a good work in you will complete it until the day of Jesus Christ;*
–Philippians 1:6 (NKJV)

Week 12

Are You in a Close, Intimate Relationship with the Holy Trinity?

Relationship - As defined in Webster's dictionary,

re·la·tion·ship

noun

1. the way in which two or more concepts, objects, or people are connected, or the state of being connected.
2. When you're in a relationship, you're emotionally involved or at least connected in some way.
3. the way in which two or more people or organizations regard and behave toward each other.

Synonyms: connection, relation, association, link, correlation, correspondence, parallel, alliance, bond, interrelation, interconnection, family ties, family connections, blood ties, blood relationship, kinship, affinity.

When you're in a relationship, you're emotionally involved or at least connected in some way. Lately, I have been focused on deepening my relationship with God, on what that looks like, and on what it means. Everything in the devotional, "Mornings with the Holy Spirit" by Jennifer LeClaire points to that and supports it through its messages. The Word itself contains many verses where Jesus invites readers to recognize that relationship is essential to living a spiritually successful life. Relationship is how new life in Christ begins.

> *"For God so loved the world, that he gave his only begotten Son, that whosoever believeth in him should not perish, but have everlasting life."*
> –John 3:16

Jesus invites and encourages relationship all throughout the Bible. The verses vary, but all of them suggest being close, near, dear, personal and intimate. Here are a few of these verses:

> *Come unto me, all ye that labor and are heavy laden, and I will give you rest.*
> –Matthew 11:28

> *Draw nigh to God, and he will draw nigh to you.*
> –James 4:8a

> *Abide in me, and I in you. As the branch cannot bear fruit of itself, except it abide in the vine; no more can ye, except ye abide in me.*
> –John 15:4

> *Behold, a virgin shall be with child, and shall bring forth a son, and they shall call his name Emmanuel, which being interpreted is, God with us.*
> –Matthew 1:23

When Jesus first called the disciples, pay attention to the words He used, and still uses today with us: *"Come and see"* and *"Follow Me."*

Let's look now at just some of the elements of a relationship:

1. It has to be two-sided. There must be at least two persons involved in any relationship. A relationship with yourself is unfruitful, narcissistic and selfish. So, fortunately, with God (the Father), Jesus (His Son) and the Holy Spirit, we have the privilege of a four-person relationship when we include ourselves! What a bonus! So, the point is, there has to be more than one person in any relationship.
2. There must be communication, be it verbal or non-verbal, physical or not. There must be some form of exchange between the persons. With God, talking and listening, or more so hearing, are vitally necessary. Without these two components, the relationship will be stale and, if neglected, non-existent. Fortunately, God tells us in Hebrews 13:5b that *"I will never leave thee, nor forsake thee."* In that, we have the assurance that He will always be there for us so that we can rekindle the relationship at any time.
3. What a comfort it is to know that God is always there, always longing for us and desiring that we engage Him in relationship. Because we are His children, even when we are not right, He pursues us and offers us the opportunity to

confess, repent and return to His loving arms. *And he arose, and came to his father. But when he was yet a great way off, his father saw him, and had compassion, and ran, and fell on his neck, and kissed him* (Luke 15:20). Do you hear the threads of relationship in that? The father's desire to restore and reconcile His relationship with his child, his son? I don't know about you, but when I think of that, it gives me great comfort.

4. There are times when I feel like God is going to cut me off because of my behavior. I must be transformed from that faulty thinking by casting down that vain imagination and by renewing my mind with what the Word says. God does not treat us the way we treat ourselves and each other. Praise God, He is so different from us! Aren't you glad that He is?!
5. So, what is your communication with God like? Do you talk to Him? Do you talk with Him? What do you say? Are you sharing how you feel, and are you being real and honest, using plain language as long as it is not vulgar or disrespectful? It's okay to be real, but we do not want to be common or unholy in our conversation with Him.
6. Are you verbalizing what you have learned from the various little life lessons? He wants to hear that from you. Are you speaking the Word back to Him, by declaring what He has said about you and the situations in your life? Do you thank Him throughout the day for things that are very personal to you which He allows

you to see and experience? The Word says, *Blessed be the Lord, who daily loadeth us with benefits…* (Psalm 68:19a). Are you listening to the little prompts He gives you? Does He ever tell you to turn this way, or don't wear that today, or to look here and you will find your keys? In my case, the Holy Spirit told me one day that my lost keys were at the curb, in the garbage bag I had just taken out! Praise God, I listened and obeyed! All of this is communication.

7. A relationship should be reciprocal—given, felt, or done in return. Now, because God loves unconditionally, He will not withhold His love when we are not pleasing to Him; however, in a relationship, even with God, we should give to Him as well. He needs nothing from us, but He desires our worship, our obedience, our praise, our faith, and our tithing. God desires our time, given not just to Him, but to others as well.
8. Are you lavishing Him with how you feel about Him, with words such as, "Oh, God, you are so good to me!" "Jesus, you are just so kind!" The relationship should have aspects of us doing something for God. And how can we do that? By obeying Him out of love and not obligation, by praying for His people, by serving others with compassion, joy and kindness. These are all ways that we can reciprocate (respond to a gesture or action by making a corresponding one).

9. Now, again, we can never match what God has done or what He continues to do for us; however, since we are in a loving relationship with Him, these acts should be a natural response to all of His goodness! As our relationship becomes more intimate, this reciprocity prayerfully will continue to grow. I submit to you, how could it not?! Our hearts would have to be like stone for us not to recognize the goodness of the Lord around us. We don't want our hearts to become so hardened that our love for God freezes!
10. Relationships should continue in growth and discovery—learning more about each other. Now, God already knows everything about us; after all, He created us before the foundation of the world and declared that we are "fearfully and wonderfully made." We should always be learning more about who He is and His attributes. This is how we come to know His magnificent names. We should take time to study Him, to experience Him and to learn more about His ways, His thoughts, His desires and His plans for our lives.
11. It is very exciting for me when I talk with friends, to learn something about them that I never knew before. One of my favorite things to do, one-on-one or with a small group of friends (outside of playing games), is to talk—just talk about how we grew up, places we have traveled to, our family life, past jobs and to explore feelings and attitudes about general topics. This is a treasure to me and something

> we need to do with our Heavenly Father, even if it is just expressing these kinds of things to Him! He loves it! This fosters communication, allowing us to discover more of who we are and who we are to Him!

As I was writing this, I had an overwhelming sense of Him as my Shepherd, my Father, my Friend, my Comforter, my Healer, my Deliverer, my Savior, my Redeemer, my Parent, my Advocate, my Counselor, my Confidant, my Champion, my Trust, my Heart, my Life and my Song! *This is relationship*!

We cannot survive without relationships. We would die—if not physically, then certainly emotionally and spiritually. We must be in relationship with one another and with God. That is the greatest commandment:

> *"Jesus said to him, 'You shall love the LORD your God with all your heart, with all your soul, and with all your mind.' This is the first and great commandment. And the second is like it: 'You shall love your neighbor as yourself.'"*
> −Matthew 22:37-39 (NKJV)

This is what the cross represents. Vertical is our love relationship with God and horizontal is our love relationship with others. God is literally the air that we breathe; we need Him, and He wants us. To neglect that relationship is to bring certain death. Just as we need water for our physical bodies, we need Jesus for spiritual life. He is the living water. Won't you engage Him in relationship today? He wants to be close to you. To "come" means to draw nearer, to move toward, move with a purpose, to advance, to go forward. Jesus is beckoning, "*Come to Me; I love you and want a relationship with you.*"

Takeaway Nugget: Have a little talk with Jesus.

Foundational Scripture: *All those the Father gives me will come to me, and whoever comes to me I will never drive away.*
–John 6:37 (NIV)

Week 13

The Greatest Party

"Girl, you missed it. Man, you shoulda been there. It was great! The best party I've ever been to."

Let me tell you about a party that you definitely do not want to miss out on. It's a birthday party for someone very special. The guest of honor's name is Jesus! It's by invitation only; however, anyone can receive one.

This is how the invitation reads:

> *'...Tell those who are invited, "See, I have prepared my dinner; my oxen and fatted cattle are killed, and all things are ready. Come to the wedding."'*
>
> –Matthew 22:4 (NKJV)

Sadly, there will be a lot of people who won't come, and this is what is said about that.

> *"The kingdom of heaven is like a king who prepared a wedding banquet for his son. He sent his servants to those who had been invited to the banquet to tell them to come, but they refused to come. But they paid no attention and went off—one to his field, another to his business. Then he said to his servants, 'The wedding banquet is ready, but those I invited did not deserve to come. So go to the street corners and invite to the banquet anyone you find.' So the servants*

> *went out into the streets and gathered all the people they could find, the bad as well as the good, and the wedding hall was filled with guests.*
> –Matthew 22:2-3, 5, 8-10 (NIV)

> *"For many are invited, but few are chosen."*
> –Matthew 22:14 (NIV)

So, getting an invitation is not a problem. However, you do need to RSVP.

> *"That if thou shalt confess with thy mouth the Lord Jesus, and shalt believe in thine heart that God hath raised him from the dead, thou shalt be saved. For with the heart man believeth unto righteousness; and with the mouth confession is made unto salvation."*
> –Romans 10:9-10

You can bring as many guests with you as you like; there's no limit.

The reason for the RSVP is to secure your reservation so that a place can be prepared for you.

> *In my Father's house are many mansions: if it were not so, I would have told you. I go to prepare a place for you. And if I go and prepare a place for you, I will come again, and receive you unto myself; that where I am, there ye may be also.*

–John 14:2-3

Cost: There is an admission fee. You can pay it now or at the door, but I highly recommend paying now because if you plan to pay at the door, it might be too late. You might not be able to get in. Just sayin'.

The cost is "a laid-down life"—where you deny your flesh and your own desires, a sacrificial life which puts Jesus and others first before your own needs. Now, that sounds like a lot, but read what is said about that.

> *So Jesus answered and said, "Assuredly, I say to you, there is no one who has left house or brothers or sisters or father or mother or wife or children or lands, for My sake and the gospel's, who shall not receive a hundredfold now in this time…"*
>
> –Mark 10:29-30a (NKJV)

Attire: Casual. Come as you are. You will receive a robe to wear though.

Gifts: You should bring a gift; it is a birthday party. It doesn't have to be elaborate, although the guest of honor is most definitely worthy of it! His yoke is easy and His burden is light; He will like whatever you bring and will graciously accept it if it's sincere.

You need to know what He likes; you can just ask any of His friends. You'll recognize them by their fruit and their title, "Redeemed Child of God." Strangers won't know what He likes. Here are some suggestions:

You can bring Him:

1. A humble and contrite heart. *The sacrifices of God are a broken spirit, A broken and a contrite heart – These, O God, You will not despise.* (Psalm 51:17 NKJV)
2. A small package of faith. He really likes mustard seeds.
3. Belts, particularly the Belt of Truth. *"Behold, You desire truth in the inward parts…"* (Psalm 51:6a NKJV)
4. Fruit. He likes most fruit, but there are nine in particular that He really likes: love, joy, peace, longsuffering, kindness, goodness, faithfulness, gentleness, self-control. If you can get them in a bundle, that would be even better. You can get them at any fruit market, but the best place is a store called Galatians. They will be the freshest if you get them from there and the fruit will abide.
5. Music. Gospel, worship music, instrumental (harp, shofar, trumpet).

Food. Dinner will be served buffet style. You can eat and drink as much as you like. You can pile your plate high and feast on all that has been prepared.

> *O taste and see that the LORD is good: blessed is the man that trusteth in Him.*
> –Psalm 34:8

There will be living bread:

"And Jesus said unto them, I am the bread of life: he that cometh to me shall never hunger; and he that believeth on me shall never thirst."
–John 6:35

Water.

Whosoever drinketh of this water shall thirst again: But whosoever drinketh of the water that I shall give him shall never thirst; but the water that I shall give him shall be in him a well of water springing up into everlasting life.
–John 4:13b-14

What you will receive:

This party is very different from any party you will ever attend. You will leave with gifts. If you come to this party, you will receive the following gifts:

1. Forgiveness of sin and relief from guilt and shame.
2. Practical help from someone who will never leave your side. Someone who will help you with all your problems and decisions. *"If you love Me, keep My commandments. And I will pray the Father, and He will give you another Helper, that He may abide with you forever – the Spirit of truth, whom the world cannot receive, because it neither sees Him nor knows Him; but you know Him, for He dwells with you and will be in you. I*

will not leave you orphans; I will come to you. (John 14:15-18 NKJV)

3. Constant companionship from Him and others. *"I will never leave thee, nor forsake thee."* (Hebrews 13:5b), *"God setteth the solitary in families…"* (Psalm 68:6a)
4. Wisdom to figure out problems by praying and asking the Holy Spirit, "How should I handle this? What's the best way to approach this problem? Where should I go—which store, which bank? Who should I ask to help me with this?"
5. Internal and eternal peace. Yes, ETERNAL.
6. Deliverance from bad habits and a dysfunctional lifestyle.
7. A friend—someone who will always tell you the truth. Someone who you can always rely on, depend on, who is always there for you. Someone who has honor and integrity; one who is genuine, kind, and tender. Someone who will always respect you, who will never put you down, make fun of you, or condemn you. Someone who loves you unconditionally. Someone who will make you feel beautiful and who will then change your sense of style to make you feel like the person you were created to be.
8. Mercy and grace. He won't count your mistakes against you when you confess them.
9. Eternal Life.

You don't want to miss this party for two main reasons:

- If you miss Jesus, you've missed everything!
- In your wanderings, you'll come to realize that life apart from living in Jesus' will and His way is futile and meaningless.

Don't miss this party! I'm going…are you coming?
Takeaway Nugget: Make sure you RSVP to Jesus' invitation.

Foundational Scripture: "*Enter by the narrow gate; for wide is the gate and broad is the way that leads to destruction, and there are many who go in by it. Because narrow is the gate and difficult is the way which leads to life, and there are few who find it.*"
–Matthew 7:13-14 (NKJV)

Week 14

I Just Don't Know What to Think!

Our thought life gets us into trouble. The bad decisions we have made and the consequences we are now suffering from began with our thoughts. We need to train our thoughts so that our actions line up with the will of God.

Romans 12:2 says it best:

> *And be not conformed to this world: but be ye transformed by the renewing of your mind, that ye may prove what is that good, and acceptable, and perfect, will of God.*

When upset or puzzled, worried, confused or just down about something, have you ever said, "I just don't know what to think?!" Well, God has given us the instruction from His Word on exactly what to think and how to renew our minds by focusing our thoughts. The Apostle Paul wrote:

> *Finally, brethren, whatsoever things are true, whatsoever things are honest, whatsoever things are just, whatsoever things are pure, whatsoever things are lovely, whatsoever things are of good report; if there be any virtue, and if there be any praise, think on these things.*
>
> –Philippians 4:8

Think: To take an inventory; estimate, conclude; count of, esteem, impute, lay, number, reason, reckon, suppose, think on

to form or have in the mind

to regard as consider

to reflect on: ponder <*think the matter over*> *b*: to determine by reflecting <*think what to do next*>

to call to mind: remember

to have as an expectation: anticipate

to center one's thoughts on *b*: to form a mental picture of

to subject to the processes of logical thought <*think things out*>

True: True, as not concealing

Honest: free of deceit and untruthfulness; sincere: reliable in accuracy or truth; true

humble, plain, or unadorned.

Just: Equitable in character or act; innocent, holy, meet, right, righteous

- dealing fairly and equally with all concerned

Pure: Clean, innocent, modest, perfect, chaste

Pure-unmixed with any other matter <*pure gold*> *(2)*:

free from dust, dirt, or taint *(3)*: spotless, stainless

Innocent-harmless in effect or intention

Chaste-pure in thought and act; severely simple in design or execution

Lovely: Friendly towards, acceptable

Dictionary:

- attractive or beautiful especially in a graceful way
- very good or likable
- very pleasing

Good report: Well-spoken of; reputable

Virtue: Manliness (valor); excellence, praise

Dictionary: morally good behavior or character; manly strength or courage

Praise: Laudation, a commendable thing

- to praise (someone or something) in a serious and often public way
- to mention (someone or something) as deserving attention or approval

Quotes:

- "Men are anxious to improve their circumstances, but are unwilling to improve themselves; they therefore remain bound." (Allen, 1903)
- "Every action and feeling is preceded by a thought." (Allen, 1903)
- "Right thinking begins with the words we say to ourselves." (Allen, 1903)
- "Circumstance does not make the man, it reveals him to himself." (Allen, 1903)

Takeaway Nugget: Are your thoughts tripping you up?

Foundational Scripture: *Set your mind on things above, not on things on the earth.*
−Colossians 3:2 (NKJV)

Week 15

Undefeated

I once listened to a man talk about the University of Michigan and its current record. He exclaimed that they were undefeated so far in that season. He spoke fondly about how great this is and that it is wonderful to see them back on top after so many difficult seasons.

The Lord began to impress upon me the spiritual parallels in all of that. I couldn't help but think later that this most definitely should be the testimony of every true follower of Christ. Our scorecard ought to read like U of M's: Body of Christ - 7; Satan - 0. We should be winning every game, no matter the opponent. We should be living from a position of "being on top despite many difficult seasons." We will definitely go through the valley of the shadow of death at times; however, the Bible tells us that,

> *Many are the afflictions of the righteous: but the LORD delivereth him out of them all.*
> –Psalm 34:19

Some seasons will be more challenging than others. We will always face trials and tests. And even if we lose the game, we still win the battle, for doesn't the Word tell us,

> *"For a just man falleth seven times, and riseth up again: but the wicked shall fall into mischief."*
> –Proverbs 24:16

Also, we are told,

> *"Be not afraid nor dismayed by reason of this great multitude; for the battle is not yours, but God's."*
>
> –2 Chronicles 20:15b

The reason we exclaim that we win the battle is that no matter what befalls us, God always works all things together for good to those who love God and are the called according to His purpose (Romans 8:28).

There is always a hash mark in the win column for us, either by way of deliverance from some habit, the working in of one of the nine fruit, the rooting out of a serious character flaw; or perhaps, the manifestation of one of God's names, increasing, strengthening and establishing us by elevating our faith as one of His attributes becomes real in our lives. The enemy means these situations for evil, but God means them for good. How can they not be good with God?!

God is greater than the enemy and anything that he dares to try to bring against us. Many times, we're our own enemy and we know that God is far greater than human clay! As I said earlier, we ought to always have the viewpoint of being on top.

> *"And the LORD will make you the head and not the tail; you shall be above only, and not be beneath, if you heed the commandments of the LORD your God, which I command you today, and are careful to observe them."*
>
> –Deuteronomy 28:13 (NKJV)

An undefeated record ought to always be the mindset and testimony of every believer. With the Holy Trinity, there are always three other people on our team. When we submit and yield to God's plan, we will always be victorious. Colossians 2:15 tells us,

> *And having spoiled principalities and powers, he made a shew of them openly, triumphing over them in it.*

What does the cross represent to you? What can your faith imagine?

In living for Christ, the cross ought to mean overcoming power, resurrected life, joy unspeakable, a way of escape, strength for the battle, staying power, feet firmly planted, unmerited favor, a constant companion, shalom and so much more! On the cross,

> *"... when Jesus had received the sour wine, He said, 'It is finished!' And bowing His head, He gave up His spirit."*
>
> –John 19:30 (NKJV)

So, the evidence is clear. We win no matter what when we are on Team Jesus! There is no defeat, no loss, no setback or losing season. As we stand with Christ, we can triumphantly declare that we are the undefeated champions and we can declare loudly, as the Michigan fight song says, that we are "victors valiant!"

Takeaway Nugget: Team Jesus for the win!

Foundational Scripture: *The LORD will cause your enemies who rise against you to be defeated before your face; they shall come out against you one way and flee before you seven ways.* –Deuteronomy 28:7 (NKJV)

Week 16

If Not Now, When?

The day after Halloween, I was scrolling through social media, looking at the various posts and was so struck by all the photos of the little kids (and adults) dressed up in various Halloween costumes. The world celebrates Halloween; so, looking at the photos, while disheartening, was not as distressing to me as the number of photos posted by Christians. As I looked at more and more photos, a sadness washed over me. I realized how many doors are being opened with this activity on young, innocent children. There are so many harmful manifestations that come from participation in such darkness, many of which may not be evident until years later. Basically, participating in Halloween is an open-door invitation to unclean spirits and demonic oppression. As I think of it now, my heart gets heavy. The day I was thinking of all this, I really did say aloud, "Oh, Lord, you must be so grieved."

Halloween, in the Christian community, is a very touchy subject. Other Christians look at you sideways when you start talking about how demonic it is and how you believe that no Christian ought to have anything to do with Halloween. Some just dismiss your comments and change the subject, but all the while, you can sense that they are silently saying, "She's weird" or "He's too serious." Others make great excuses about how harmless it is—how cute the kids look, how they host a party at their church so that at least that way, they know the kids are safe; or, that it's okay because we dress them in sweet little costumes like angels or superheroes—nothing demonic. No matter what you might say or what passages of Scripture you might throw out as evidence of God's position, there is no convincing them that this is not an activity in which Christians ought to participate. And some even go so far as to say, "Where in the Bible does it say we shouldn't celebrate Halloween?"

My stance on Halloween is not a self-righteous one; it is one of deep conviction, which I embraced after being taught about it and after reading a book about the history, purpose and origins of the so-called "holiday." Many people simply do not know about Halloween and its dark origins, so their embracing of it is understandable. Unfortunately, many churches today are not taking on challenging topics and are just placating the ears of those who show up in their pews. We need to be challenged in our walk.

There will be times when the pastor speaks about long-standing historical behaviors or practices that are no longer befitting of a Christian. I remember one of my ministry sisters saying, "It no longer fits." When we become a new creature in Christ, many habits, attitudes, ideas, behaviors, associates, friendships and practices no longer represent the new person we have become. There are just some things we have to give up. The interesting thing is that because Jesus gives us a new heart, we no longer actually desire some of these things! Our desires change as the sanctification process takes place and continues. Truthfully, if that is not happening, then it's probably time for a heart check.

The problem is that some of us Christians do not want to change.

We don't want to give up some of those old, worldly practices, but we must if we are to grow in the knowledge of the Lord and be conformed into His image. We must crucify the old man and put on the new man.

> *"But you have not so learned Christ, if indeed you have heard Him and have been taught by Him, as the truth is in Jesus: that you put off, concerning your former conduct, the old man which grows corrupt according to the deceitful lusts, and be renewed in the spirit of your mind, and that you put on the new man which was created according to God, in true righteousness and holiness."*
>
> –Ephesians 4:20-24 (NKJV)

It's hard to change, but with the help of the Holy Spirit, it is possible, doable and necessary. We just have to be willing. Our minds must be renewed by reading the Word. Then, we have to submit our will to the Father's will. The good news though, is that we don't have to make the change—we cannot do so anyway. He will bring about the change in us as we allow Him to continue the work He started. As we yield to the working of the Holy Spirit, the change will surely come, little by little.

> *But we all, with unveiled face, beholding as in a mirror the glory of the Lord, are being transformed into the same image from glory to glory, just as by the Spirit of the Lord.*
>
> –2 Corinthians 3:18 (NKJV)

One thing I have learned and experienced in my walk is that our Lord is gracious. He is not harsh or demanding of His children, but gentle and kind. He wants to see us delivered, healed and whole so that He can use us! How can He do that if we refuse to conform to His standards of what is righteous and holy? How can we say that we love Him if we do not obey His commands? How can we continue to participate in unholy activities that bring no glory to God?

Let me throw out some words. Think about the meaning of each one as you read them: Dark, demonic, evil, wicked, vile, malevolent, impish, naughty, satanic, occult…

Parents dress up their children as monsters, vampires, devils, witches and ghosts, and encourage them to approach total strangers to ask them for candy and other treats. Homeowners decorate their houses with images of black cats, ghosts, goblins and carved pumpkins. Sometimes, they will transform their front yards into make-believe graveyards. Adults dress in strange and often outlandish costumes and attend parties that are decorated like dungeons or crypts. How can we look at such images and say, "Oh, isn't that cute?"

Christians celebrating Halloween is an *oxymoron*, which means ideas or terms that are combined that are opposite or contradictory. For example, "jumbo shrimp," "original copy," "sweet sorrow." "Christians and Halloween." There is just no justification or argument for Christians celebrating Halloween. There are so many Scriptures that are clear on the distinction between good and evil, light and dark, and living godly versus living worldly. Here are a few:

Love not the world, neither the things that are in the world. If any man love the world, the love of the Father is not in him. For all that is in the world, the lust of the flesh, and the lust of the eyes, and the pride of life, is not of the Father, but is of the world. And the world passeth away, and the lust thereof: but he that doeth the will of God abideth forever.
—1 John 2:15-17

When you enter the land the LORD your God is giving you, do not learn to imitate the detestable ways of the nations there. Let no one be found among you who sacrifices their son or daughter in the fire, who practices divination or sorcery, interprets omens, engages in witchcraft, or casts spells, or who is a medium or spiritist or who consults the dead. Anyone who does these things is detestable to the LORD; because of these same detestable practices the LORD your God will drive out those nations before you. You must be blameless before the LORD your God.
—Deuteronomy 18:9-13 (NIV)

And there are so, so many more!

Okay, so this topic is a no-brainer; it's not rocket science. It's pretty clear. The problem is it's something adults enjoy and many just want to keep doing it. So, now you know.

Therefore to him that knoweth to do good, and doeth it not, to him it is sin.
–James 4:17

Children are taught. Those who don't grow up celebrating Halloween don't care about it. Children have to be instructed. They learn behavior and practices.

The next time Halloween approaches, meditate on this topic and let the Holy Spirit speak to you. If you or someone you know is still not convicted, now is the time to cry out to the Lord and ask Him to work on your/their heart. He is willing and able to renew your minds and give your flesh an assist.

There are, of course, other works of the flesh that we deal with daily, which hopefully, all of us are crying out to the Lord about. Halloween, however, is a big deal in our world today—a financially top-grossing "holiday" that Christians are still celebrating!

I can't help but think about the damage being done to our children as doors to unclean spirits are opened up to them. There is so much that is dark that opens up doors and we never make the connection. There can be so many manifestations related to dabbling in the spirit realm, and that's not just Halloween. We can cite horror movies, psychics, tarot cards, horoscopes, mythology, and the list goes on. People are unaware of the effects of exposing themselves to these things, but here are some examples for both adults and children: Illness, recurring illness with no basis, undiagnosed symptoms, problems concentrating in school, difficulty with homework, nightmares, depression, anxiety, tics, migraines, fear, bedwetting, aggression, insomnia, night terrors, unwanted nighttime visitations, panic attacks and much more. Of course, there are many contributing factors to these kinds of things, but being aware of what you expose yourself to, open doors to and involve yourself in is very important.

I am passionate about this because I have experienced it firsthand, so I know what I am talking about. I was not saved as a child, teen or young adult. Many doors were opened to me, albeit, unknowingly, by what I was exposed to—certain music (e.g., pop/rock), Ouija boards, celebrating Halloween and so much more. Unclean spirits tormented me in the night, as I sometimes woke up gasping for air as though I was being suffocated. Because of those opened doors, those spirits had legal access to attack me. I know that many people do not believe or understand this kind of experience, but it is real and is ruining the lives of Christians, both children and adults.

I can sense the grief that Jesus must feel as He watches His people participating in the demonic activity going on in our world. This is far too broad a topic to delve into here, but if you sense the Holy Spirit leading you to gain a deeper understanding, please do not ignore it. Pray and ask Him to guide you into the truth.

Our children are precious; the Bible says,

> *Lo, children are an heritage of the* L*ORD*: *and the fruit of the womb is his reward.*
> –Psalm 127:3

As adults, we cannot continue to expose them to darkness and expect either them or us to be blessed and to prosper. There are consequences to courting darkness in any form. Those effects may not show up right away, but they will, to be sure.

In general, it's time to live our faith. It's past time. This message isn't meant to be a guilt trip; it's not about condemnation, but about conviction. The enemy condemns; Jesus convicts. We need to practice what we say we believe and make small changes day by day. Christians, those called by His name, and who say they love the Lord, must awaken, study, read the Word, walk in the light and desire truth in the inward parts. It's time to do this; and if not now, when?

Prayer

Dear Heavenly Father,

I pray this prayer in the name of Jesus. I confess and admit that in my ignorance, I've fully participated in Halloween. I know now that this practice is demonic, and I ask You to forgive me for grieving the Holy Spirit by participating in something so evil. Forgive me for grieving You by my past or current involvement in Halloween. Having had my mind renewed by hearing the truth about it, I denounce and renounce Halloween and everything associated with it right here, right now. I turn from that practice and embrace your holiness in all areas of my life.

Holy Spirit, I sincerely desire to know about any other things in my past and present, in which I have participated that have not brought You the glory and honor You deserve. Please reveal those areas to me so I can turn from those as well. And now, Father, I receive your forgiveness and close the door to those activities and the mindset. I thank You for this opportunity to be filled with the knowledge of Your will in all wisdom and spiritual understanding, that I may walk worthy of the Lord, fully pleasing You, being fruitful in every good work and increasing in the knowledge of God. In Jesus' name, I pray! Amen!

Takeaway Nugget: Search your heart and research Halloween and its origin.

Foundational Scripture: *And have no fellowship with the unfruitful works of darkness, but rather reprove them.*
–Ephesians 5:11

Week 17

Rules to Live By

Live beneath your means.
Return everything you borrow.
Stop blaming other people.
Admit it when you make a mistake.
Give clothes not worn to charity.
Do something nice and try not to get caught.
Listen more; talk less.
Everyday take a 30-minute walk.
Strive for excellence, not perfection.
Be on time.
Don't make excuses.
Don't argue.
Get organized.
Be kind to people.
Be kind to unkind people.
Let someone cut ahead of you in line.
Take time to be alone.
Cultivate good manners.
Be humble.
Realize and accept that life isn't fair.
Know when to keep your mouth shut.
Go an entire day without criticizing anyone.
Learn from the past.

Plan for the future.
Live in the present.
Don't sweat the small stuff. It's all small stuff."
–From a Quaker newsletter

When I read the above quote, I found scriptural support for each rule.

1. **Live beneath your means.**
   Take heed and beware of covetousness, for one's life does not consist in the abundance of the things he possesses.
   –Luke 12:15 (NKJV)

2. **Return everything you borrow.**
   If you ever take your neighbor's garment as a pledge, you shall return it to him before the sun goes down.
   –Exodus 22:26 (NKJV)

3. **Stop blaming other people.**
   And why do you look at the speck in your brother's eye, but do not consider the plank in your own eye? Or how can you say to your brother, 'Let me remove the speck from your eye'; and look, a plank is in your own eye? Hypocrite! First remove the plank from your own eye, and then you will see clearly to remove the speck from your brother's eye.
   –Matthew 7:3-5 (NKJV)

4. **Admit it when you make a mistake.**

   He who covers his sins will not prosper, But whoever confesses and forsakes them will have mercy.

   –Proverbs 28:13 (NKJV)

5. **Give clothes not worn to charity.**

   Whoever is generous to the poor lends to the LORD, and he will repay him for his deed.

   –Proverbs 19:17 (ESV)

6. **Do something nice and try not to get caught.**

   Take heed that you do not do your charitable deeds before men, to be seen by them. Otherwise you have no reward from your Father in heaven.

   –Matthew 6:1 (NKJV)

7. **Listen more; talk less.**

   So then, my beloved brethren, let every man be swift to hear, slow to speak, slow to wrath;

   –James 1:19 (NKJV)

8. **Everyday take a 30-minute walk.**

   Or do you not know that your body is a temple of the Holy Spirit within you, whom you have from God? You are not your own, for you were bought with a price. So glorify God in your body.

   –1 Corinthians 6:19-20 (ESV)

9. **Strive for excellence, not perfection.**

   And whatever you do, do it heartily, as to the Lord and not to men.

   –Colossians 3:23 (NKJV)

10. **Be on time.**

    To every thing there is a season, and a time to every purpose under the heaven:

    –Ecclesiastes 3:1

    Commentary tells us, "Time is important. The secret to peace with God is to discover, accept, and appreciate God's perfect timing."

11. **Don't make excuses.**

    He said to him, "Do you want to be made well?" The sick man answered Him, "Sir, I have no man to put me into the pool when the water is stirred up; but while I am coming, another steps down before me." Jesus said to him, "Rise, take up your bed and walk." And immediately the man was made well, took up his bed, and walked.

    –John 5:6b-9 (NKJV)

12. **Don't argue.**

    If it is possible, as much as depends on you, live peaceably with all men.

    –Romans 12:18 (NKJV)

13. Get organized.

Let all things be done decently and in order.
–1 Corinthians 14:40 (NKJV)

14. Be kind to people.

And be kind to one another, tenderhearted, forgiving one another, even as God in Christ forgave you.
–Ephesians 4:32 (NKJV)

15. Be kind to unkind people.

But I say to you who hear: Love your enemies, do good to those who hate you, bless those who curse you, and pray for those who spitefully use you.
–Luke 6:27-28 (NKJV)

16. Let someone cut ahead of you in line.

Be kindly affectionate to one another with brotherly love, in honor giving preference to one another;
–Romans 12:10 (NKJV)

17. Take time to be alone.

And in the morning, rising up a great while before day, he went out, and departed into a solitary place, and there prayed.
–Mark 1:35

18. Cultivate good manners.

And just as you want men to do to you, you also do to them likewise.

–Luke 6:31 (NKJV)

19. Be humble.

Humble yourselves in the sight of the Lord, and He will lift you up.

–James 4:10 (NKJV)

20. Realize and accept that life isn't fair.

The LORD executes righteousness and justice for all who are oppressed.

–Psalm 103:6 (NKJV)

21. Know when to keep your mouth shut.

A fool vents all his feelings, but a wise man holds them back.

–Proverbs 29:11 (NKJV)

22. Go an entire day without criticizing anyone.

Judge not, that you be not judged.

–Matthew 7:1 (NKJV)

23. Learn from the past.

For everything that was written in the past was written to teach us, so that through the endurance taught in the Scriptures and the encouragement they provide we might have hope.

—Romans 15:4 (NIV)

24. Plan for the future.

In all thy ways acknowledge Him, and He shall direct thy paths.

—Proverbs 3:6

25. Live in the present.

Therefore do not worry about tomorrow, for tomorrow will worry about its own things. Sufficient for the day is its own trouble.

—Matthew 6:34 (NKJV)

26. Don't sweat the small stuff. It's all small stuff.

Be anxious for nothing…

—Philippians 4:6a (NKJV)

Takeaway Nugget: Live by the rules of God's Word.

Foundational Scripture: *All Scripture is given by inspiration of God, and is profitable for doctrine, for reproof, for correction, for instruction in righteousness, that the man of God may be complete, thoroughly equipped for every good work.*

—2 Timothy 3:16-17 (NKJV)

Week 18

Stuck in a Groove

Remember the days of vinyl records when the needle would get stuck in a groove, and the record would skip in the same place over and over?

Mary had a, had a, had a, had a, had a, had a…

Nothing would stop it from doing that except human intervention. It could go on like that for hours. Someone had to pick up the needle and move it forward. Aren't we just like this sometimes? Sometimes, we just get stuck in a groove and it could be year after year after year that we are doing the exact same thing.

One definition of insanity is "doing the same thing over and over, and expecting different results." I'm not willing to call any of you insane, but let's just say that sometimes, you and I just get "stuck on stupid." And that's the last time I'm going to use that word, but you know what I'm talking about. We're still practicing the same habits, still having the same old conversation, still harboring the same feelings of unforgiveness and still being undisciplined with our finances; yet, we're wondering why things are so tight. We really need help!

Similar to the record, we need someone to intervene, and in this case, it's going to take divine intervention to get our needle out of the groove and move forward.

Purpose to come out of your rut. Start by remembering first what God says in His Word.

> *Therefore if any man be in Christ, he is a new creature: old things are passed away; behold, all things are become new.*
> –2 Corinthians 5:17

Those words right there should be the encouragement you need to get started. He will make a road in the wilderness and rivers in the desert. God wants to do something new in your life. He's just waiting for that. He has already done everything that He is going to do; now, it's up to you.

One thing I have learned about the Lord is that He is faithful. He has helped me in every challenging situation, big or small, and has either removed it, taught me something about it, revealed something about myself or has shown me an aspect of His character and attributes. This only strengthened my faith and brought me into a closer relationship with Him. He's a faithful God; He brings us through. I like this catchphrase, which is a comforting reminder: "So far, you have survived 100% of your worst days."

Let's look at some practical ways that you can get unstuck. You must do something different. Try these suggestions:

Perhaps you're having difficulty reading your Bible. You want to get into the Word, but reading it is a challenge. First, ask the Holy Spirit to give you the desire to read it. Then, try listening to it on audio. There are plenty of free audio versions that you can listen to—some apps even offer dramatic readings!

You don't seem to have enough time in the day to get your reading in. Read for 10 minutes in the morning, 10 minutes at lunchtime and 10 minutes in the evening.

Set your alarm for each scheduled reading. Look! That's 30 minutes for the day! That's even how we're told to get in our exercise. Don't be hard on yourself. Start with small steps.

> *There is therefore now no condemnation to them which are in Christ Jesus, who walk not after the flesh, but after the Spirit.*
> –Romans 8:1

You've got a problem that you're worrying about, and can't seem to stop worrying. Every time you find yourself worrying about that problem, *stop.* Catch yourself, and then alphabetically begin to thank the Lord for something. Start with the letter A and go all the way through to Z. Doing so will take your mind off your problem while offering up thanksgiving to God!

You are upset or angry with someone. Force yourself to write down 10 good things about that person. Don't do it in your head. Get a pen, write them down and read each item. Ask God to help you forgive that person. The Bible says,

> *"Bless them which persecute you: bless, and curse not.*
> –Romans 12:14

In one of my Bible commentaries, *bless* means "to speak well of or praise." It also means to pray for them. So, even if you can't pray for them, you can find something nice to say about them.

The point of all of this is that you've got to start somewhere. You're in a rut and don't want to stay there.

The good news is that you don't have to. The Holy Spirit, our Helper, is more than willing to empower you to move forward. He is there to help and wants to do it. Ask Him; then, do something. Sometimes, you have to cut back, cut out, cut off, get rid of, start, stop, begin, end, reconsider, rethink, reevaluate, and just make a change. Stop making excuses.

Purpose in your heart that you are going to do a new thing in the Lord. Purpose means *to propose as an aim to oneself.* It also means *to have as one's intention or objective.* Do something different and, in the words of a very excited little boy in a video who was anticipating baptism, "Just do it."

Takeaway Nugget: You've got to start somewhere.

Foundational Scripture: *When Jesus saw him lying there, and knew that he already had been in that condition a long time, He said to him, "Do you want to be made well?"*
–John 5:6 (NKJV)

Week 19

A and D Ointment

Forgiveness is the ointment that needs to be applied to certain wounds in you. It opens you up and releases the ability for you to see the other person in a different light. As you yield, you begin to see the pain of their life (because there is always a deep-seated, deep-rooted need in *that* person that has caused them to wound you, or your perception of a wound; otherwise, you wouldn't be in a position of having to forgive them). Think about it. The only reason you're having to forgive them is that they've said or done something that hurt you, or that you perceived they've said or done something. So, something is wrong in their soul to have caused their action against you. They are hurting. They have been wounded or else they need salvation desperately; you wouldn't be in a position to forgive them.

Most people—unless they are psychopaths or sociopaths—don't just wake up every day and purposely say, "Okay! Let's see who I can attack and deeply wound today." The fiery darts that the average person hurls at you or someone else with their words or in their actions all come from a place of deep, unresolved, buried, unprocessed, unrevealed pain, need and longing.

The ointment of forgiveness is what opens you up to see that. But first, you have to apply it. Where do you get this ointment? You have to ask for it, but only one person has it: the Holy Spirit. You have to go to Him to get it. I'm sure you've seen this ointment before. It comes in a tube sold in every pharmacy. However, in this analogy, A and D stands for "Anointing and Deliverance." It's named that because it takes the Holy Spirit's anointing to come upon you to forgive. As you yield to it, deliverance comes forth in you as you're released from the prison of unforgiveness.

Now, this ointment is *very* powerful; you only need to apply just a little. Squeeze out just a tiny bit, apply it directly to your heart and massage it in. This releases the anointing for you to say (for example), "I choose to forgive my father for never once telling me he loved me or was proud of me." You must be specific by naming the "offender" and stating specifically what the offense is. You may be saying or thinking, "Oh, no, I can't do that." And you're right—*you* can't. Remember this: it's the anointing from the Holy Spirit that empowers you to choose to forgive and speak words of forgiveness. That's when the deliverance of your soul begins. The Holy Spirit can now begin the work.

You may not see it or feel anything; you probably won't. That opening up of you begins because God is working. Since you walk by faith and not by sight, you will soon begin to see that other person in a different light. Most importantly, you'll begin to see *yourself* differently and the part you played in all of this.

You may say or think, "My part? They hurt *me*!"

Yes, your part. Any time someone wrongs you or you allow yourself to be hurt, wounded, or offended, your heart now becomes hardened. This can lead to the bitterness you've been nursing and the thoughts and feelings you've harbored all this time, locking you in the prison of unforgiveness. Think of all the energy you've spent thinking nasty thoughts and making unkind remarks to yourself (and others) about the person. Think about all the complaining you've done about the person. Think about how you've replayed the scenario over and over, rehearsing what was said, if you even remember it, and then all the ways you've shut yourself off from the person by not speaking to them or through your body language and your own actions. Think about all the plans you've made to pay them back and how elaborate those plans have become. That's exhausting! Yes, your part!

Do you really think Jesus is okay with all that? Of course, He's not! In case you're having trouble with that, read the following Scriptures.

> *Bless those who persecute you; bless and do not curse. Repay no one evil for evil. If it is possible, as much as depends on you, live peaceably with all men.*
>
> −Romans 12:14, 17a, 18 (NKJV)

> *Let no corrupt word proceed out of your mouth…Let all bitterness, wrath, anger, clamor, and evil speaking be put away from you, with all malice. And be kind to one another, tenderhearted, forgiving one another, even as God in Christ forgave you.*
>
> −Ephesians 4:29, 31-32 (NKJV)

So, yes—*your part*!

As the Holy Spirit brings to your mind and heart all of the things you have thought, said or done to contribute to this "standoff," hopefully, deliverance is happening!

You should be getting a whole new picture and conviction from what the Word says about forgiving others, which should be pulling on you big time!

You must want to be free. You have to take the first step and admit your part. You must first tell the Lord, "I have not wanted to forgive this person; I have stayed locked in this prison all this time. But now, I want to come out." When you do that, the Holy Spirit is standing there, ready to come to your aid and help you speak out your forgiveness declaration. Go and get yourself some A and D ointment, and speak forgiveness out audibly *today*.

Now, let me read to you what it says on the tube.

- Widely recommended by pastors, ministers and churches
- Fast, soothing relief for:
    - Insult rash
    - Chafed emotions
    - Resentment abrasions
    - Minor offenses
- A and D Ointment aids the healing process.

When applied sparingly, it forms an enemy-proof protective barrier against many people irritants. Apply as needed or consult Jehovah Rapha.

Ingredients: Balm of Gilead, Fish Liver Oil, Pleasing Fragrance, Paraffin and Sweet-smelling Aroma

You can find this anywhere, at any store where faith is sold. There is no cost for it, but you do have to ask for it. It is freely given. Use it as often as you need to because forgiveness is a process. There is an endless supply and this formula is called 70 X 7. That's because this is how many times Jesus says you should forgive.

> *"Then came Peter to him, and said, Lord, how oft shall my brother sin against me, and I forgive him? till seven times? Jesus saith unto him, I say not unto thee, Until seven times: but, Until seventy times seven.*
> –Matthew 18:21-22

And while that adds up to 490 times, it's symbolic, since seven and seventy represent completion and perfection. So, in essence, we are to forgive completely and perfectly, and that adds up to all the time!

After you make your forgiveness declaration, you must ask the Holy Spirit to "now, please work it in my heart." Every time you apply the ointment to your heart, you must massage it in. Once it's massaged in, the Holy Spirit comes along and really begins to do the inner healing work.

In our example, the situation involving the father and son is serious, but not all offenses are that serious. Some are the little foxes that keep you bound. A co-worker may not speak to you when you say good morning and you don't know why. You might begin to develop an attitude and say things like, "Well, I'm just not going to say 'good morning' anymore. If he's not going to speak to me, I won't speak to him." Then bitterness sets in. You know how you are. It's possible he has a hearing deficit and didn't hear you. We are too easily offended and too quick to make assumptions. We have to learn to forgive. We have to learn to let things go.

Remember, as you yield, the Holy Spirit works. It's in this work that you begin to open up to see that person in a different light. In our one example, you begin to see that your father never had anyone to tell him that he was loved or that anyone was proud of him. In fact, all he heard from his caregivers (parents, older siblings) was that he was a disappointment and that he would never amount to anything. There was cursing and name-calling, and he never saw anyone model loving behavior. And although he loved you, he didn't know how to tell you or encourage you. No one ever taught him. As the Holy Spirit massages your heart, you begin to see this, and your heart begins to soften toward your father.

The D part of the ointment (the deliverance) begins to open you up to seeing that your father wasn't a bad person at all. In fact, he had many good qualities; you just never noticed them before. Why? Because you can't see good things through your own bitterness. It's like looking through a dirty, clouded window every day. If someone asks you what you see through it, you might say, "I see dirt and cloudy smears." But once that dirt is wiped off (by the Holy Spirit in the process), you can see the sunshine, the children playing and laughing outside, and all the good things that are just outside the window. They have been there all along; the bitterness you harbored blocked your view—blocked your perspective because all you could focus on was the dirt and smears on the window.

Allow this to sink in: "Those good things, those good qualities in that other person have been there all along." Yielding to the process of forgiveness opens your eyes to see what you never noticed before. Your heart begins to soften; now, truth can come in and show you another view. Even if the person's actions never change, you do and you get a freedom that is priceless! Forgiveness is the key to releasing you from all the turmoil, unrest and torment that's going on in the inner workings of your soul.

One thing I have learned is that spiritual matters are not black and white; what you see is not always the obvious cause and effect. In our natural world, if you drop something, it falls to the ground because of gravity. That's pretty black and white. But you don't always see what's going on with you spiritually. It could be that your sleepless nights are caused by holding on to unforgiveness. You may not make that connection. Your inability to get that promotion at work could be due to unforgiveness. Just as God is doing an inner work, so is the enemy doing an inner work in your soul to keep you bound, to keep you uptight, angry, stubborn and full of pride so that you won't yield to the process of forgiveness.

"You just don't know what they did to me," you may say.

No, we don't. And you may have truly experienced something terrible or traumatic, but what are you going to do? You're going to live out the rest of your days angry and bitter over what someone did or said to you weeks—maybe months or years ago. Is it worth sacrificing your intimate relationship with Jesus? There's a purpose in everything we experience and God has a plan for it. Yes, it hurts. It was painful—awful even when you experienced it. But God brought you through it so He can make something beautiful and redeemable out of it—if you will allow Him to.

Open your eyes and your heart today, and ask God who you need to forgive. If you are truly honest with yourself, you probably already know or have an inkling. Take that inkling, which is a slight tug from the Holy Spirit, and ask Him to help you make your declaration of forgiveness today. Then praise Him for the help and the deliverance that will follow. Trust that He will help you release it all and then reveal to you how He wants to redirect that pain. He wants to use your struggle to help someone else! Now is the time to sing a new song. It's time. Get started today!

Takeaway Nugget: Forgiveness unlocks you.

Foundational Scripture: *For if ye forgive men their trespasses, your heavenly Father will also forgive you: But if ye forgive not men their trespasses, neither will your Father forgive your trespasses.*
–Matthew 6:14-15

Week 20

Knock, Knock. Who's There?

There's a young woman in my life who's in her 30s. One day, she said to me, "It's bad; my anxiety is through the roof." Because I know her, I know that she is struggling greatly and is having a hard time managing aspects of her life because of the anxiety. I didn't have much to minister to her in that specific moment, but I told her to get into the Word. Later, I reflected on what another person said: "I wonder if it's who she's been around." I nodded in understanding and went on with my day.

I have been praying for the young woman. More recently, after she made the remark about her anxiety, I have asked the Lord how to pray for her. I was reminded of something I read in the book, Psalm 23, The Song of a Passionate Heart. It was one tiny statement that made a huge impact on me: "The marks of Satan's presence are anxiety." That leaped off the page at me when I read it. I remember thinking, *well, I certainly do not want to invoke the presence of Satan.* I had never really thought about it that way, as actually invoking his presence. I meditated on that greatly and am still using that statement as a tool to remind myself that when I feel anxious, I need to stop and do whatever I need to do to invoke the presence of God.

I know anxiety. I was the "poster child" for anxiety and panic attacks, but God supernaturally delivered me from that manifestation of the spirit of fear through the teachings of the ministry and church to which I belong. Those teachings helped my understanding of how the enemy attacks us. God taught me how to overcome it and gave me understanding so that I would be built up to fight it.

Through my teachings, I learned that I was dealing with an unclean spirit that was trying to overtake me. I had never heard of such a thing. The more I researched and studied, I got a greater understanding. When I read one of the definitions of anxiety, the fight was on. I had read definitions of anxiety and when my eyes fell upon this—[from the Early 17th century Latin *anxius*< *anx-*, past participle of *angere,* which means "torment," literally "strangle"], Oh, it was on! I still remember my reaction. I sat up strong and said, "Oh, no; I don't think so!" That spirit was trying to take me out!

So, where is God taking us today with all of this? The young woman said, "My anxiety is through the roof." The quote I cited earlier from the book said, "The marks of Satan's presence are anxiety." Therefore, we must delve deeper and ask God to reveal to us how we might be invoking Satan's presence.

Whenever you experience anxiety, worry, stress or anything that disturbs your peace, the Holy Trinity is not in that picture. Why? Because Jesus is peace. So, He is not present in any of that. I remember one day, a close friend saw me running around, trying to gather up this and that, exclaiming that I was going to be late. She walked up to me and said, "Audrey, stop. Just stop for a minute and breathe. Listen to this: 'God is not in a hurry.'"

"I know; I know," I said.

"No," she spoke slowly. "Listen. 'God is not in a hurry.'"

"You're right; you're right, He's not."

"You're not getting it." And then, the light bulb came on, and I heard it. "God is not in a hurry." The message was that God is not *present* in a hurry—in a rush. His presence is not in that. He's not near. So, whose presence is? The enemy's, of course! "The marks of Satan's presence are anxiety."

So, now let's go back and go even further. How does Satan even get into our presence? We invite him in. Of course, we would say, "Oh, no, I'm not inviting Satan's presence in." However, we do so unknowingly. We need to understand how we do it.

When you're at home and someone knocks at the door or rings the bell, you get up to go see who it is. Generally, if you don't know the person, you don't open the door; therefore, they do not gain entrance into your home. But what happens when even though you don't really know the person, you let them step in—even just a little, right across the threshold. Then you may discover you're talking with someone you wished you had not let in. What did you do? You opened the door to an unwanted intruder!

We open doors every day without knowing it. We need to be more thoughtful, conscious, and discerning about who we open the door to. These intruders, unclean spirits, come in many forms; we must take the time to be more discerning.

One day, I was in a small shop. Normally, you'll hear relaxing music or no music at all. However, on this particular day, the music was blaring and the beat was bumping and thumping. Although the words were not profane, they were attacking my spirit. I do not listen to that particular genre of music and I was vexed. I immediately asked for that music to be turned off or to find something else more soothing.

The point is this: a door was opened. I didn't purposely open it, but the attack came in. What might you be listening to? What are your children or grandchildren listening to? We all know that music gets into your spirit and stays there. We remember lyrics from our old man days, especially the sensual lyrics that we sang. Unholy lyrics from days in our past sometimes just come to mind. Next thing we know, we're singing along or humming the tune and we don't know why. Perhaps the song was playing somewhere in the background. It doesn't matter; somehow, it got into your spirit (open door). So, I ask you again, "What are you listening to? What's getting into your spirit?" Also, you have to consider the author of the music. What are they or were they into? Were they on mind-altering drugs when they wrote the lyrics? That's highly possible.

Many of the people I listened to growing up were probably under the influence of some substance while writing or recording their music. What are the lyrics saying? If the presence of God or something genuinely wholesome or innocent is not in those lyrics, your spirit could be vexed. Remember, you are trying to determine possible causes for your anxiety, stress, and physical or emotional sensations. Ask yourself:

What did I invite in?

Where have I been in the last few days?

Was I around an anxious, negative person?

Do I live with one?

What influence has that person had on me as I watched their fearful, worrisome behavior, and listened to their negative comments?

Who are you dating? What spirits are on them that may be transferring to you? If you are involved with a depressed person with low self-esteem, the spirit on them can overtake *you* if you don't know who you are and are not built up in the Word. Maybe you hugged someone in a deep embrace and later on, you felt different—a little down or sad. The unclean spirit on them may have transferred to you—open door.

Now, before you get all bent out of shape, that doesn't mean that you should never hug anyone again or get all religious and say, "Oh, no, I better not hug them." That's not what this is about. It's about being more aware, more discerning, and seeking the Holy Spirit about the people you associate with, those you are around, spend time with and have much association with. If you are unable to avoid such people, then ask the Holy Spirit how to prepare yourself before being in their presence so that you are not overtaken by what's in or on them. Maybe you should pray in your spirit language on the way to their home. And that brings us to another point.

Where are you spending time? What physical places have you gone into? Are you in environments that do not have the presence of God? Have you been in a nightclub? Have you been in an art gallery or art marketplace? I mention this due to my own experience. Let me share this brief testimony.

I once went into a local art marketplace in my hometown. I had never been in there before. As I walked through the marketplace, all seemed innocent at first. But as I ventured farther and farther into the space, my spirit began to pick up on something. I took notice of the art and other creations that were laced with darkness—skulls, pictures of devils, dark images of sad faces, even some artwork with profanity. Now that my eyes were wide open, I could sense the heaviness, loneliness and despair in that place. I couldn't get out of there fast enough. Once I got outside, it was pouring rain and I had no umbrella, but I didn't care. I just pressed on to my car.

Audibly, I was confessing and repenting to the Lord for going in there. I began to declare over myself that "no weapon formed against me (from here) shall prosper" and I pled the blood of Jesus over myself and began to denounce any unclean spirit that might have tried to attach itself to me. You don't always notice this sort of thing at first. You must be in tune to your surroundings, especially as a child of God.

Maybe you were in the casino? And no, that may not be your sort of thing, but you were in the environment. What is going on in a casino? Gambling, which can be an addiction for many people. So, the spirit of addiction is in the air. Drinking (usually in excess), loss of inhibition and self-control; the obsession with winning money, so a possible spirit of whoredoms (which is greed) are all in the air. And while you may not be gambling, you're in a place where the door is open, and you have just invited unclean spirits in.

Certain books, TV news, glitz and glamour magazines, tabloids with so much negativity and inflated stories (lying spirit), and horror movies can all have an effect on your spirit. Sometimes, in art galleries/marketplaces, you can see the darkness in some of the drawings and paintings. Again, having experienced this, I had to leave an art marketplace I was in where the pictures were so dark and gothic, with skeletons and other demonic imagery. As I walked through, I could sense my mood changing; I could feel the sadness, the emptiness and the need for Jesus; the cries for help, and the pain of the artists. It was too much. And had not my spirit been discerning, I might have walked through there, lollygagging along, not realizing that a door was being opened. Hours later, I might not have made the connection that a door had been opened while wondering, "Why am I feeling so down, so heavy?" All of these things have the potential to get into your spirit and affect your mood, behavior and how you are feeling (anxious, tense, stressed or even unmotivated).

This topic can get very deep spiritually and it needs to be further delved into, but I do not have the time. However, the Lord wants you to consider what you are exposing yourself to and what you have already opened the door to and invited into your mind, your spirit, your home and your life. There is a connection to how you are feeling and what you have been exposed to. We don't always notice it or see it immediately; sometimes not at all, until it is pointed out. However, it's worth meditating on and seeking the Holy Spirit about. Ask Him. Ask Him to reveal to you what and who you are consorting with.

Now, be cautioned: you have to stay in balance. Not everything you encounter is a "door opener." Do not go too far to one end or the other. The Holy Spirit is a temperate, reasonable, disciplined, balanced person. Seek Him to keep all of this in perspective so you don't become religious about it, refusing to hug people after service or never going into certain places! All things in moderation and thoughtfulness.

We have to guard our spirit. We must guard our gates and what goes into them—eyes, ears, and mouth.

> *My son, pay attention to what I say; turn your ear to my words. Do not let them out of your sight, keep them within your heart; for they are life to those who find them and health to one's whole body. Above all else, guard your heart, for everything you do flows from it. Keep your mouth free of perversity; keep corrupt talk far from your lips. Let your eyes look straight ahead; fix your gaze directly before you. Give careful thought to the paths for your feet and be steadfast in all your ways. Do not turn to the right or the left; keep your foot from evil.*
> –Proverbs 4:20-27 (NIV)

Now, what is the solution, once you have opened the door and your unwanted guest is in the house? You must invite him to leave. Even if he is stubborn about going, you have the right to kick him out. Go to the Father, in the name of Jesus, and first confess that you let this intruder in. Then get out the sword of the Spirit (the Word, of course) and begin to declare the opposite of what has tried to infiltrate your home and your spirit. Find Scriptures that counteract what you are now feeling. For anxiety, find Scriptures on peace.

"Thou wilt keep Him in perfect peace whose mind is stayed on Thee."
–Isaiah 26:3

"Be still and know that I am God."
–Psalm 46:10

"I cast all my anxiety on Him because He cares for me."
–1 Peter 5:7

Begin to declare who you are in Christ. "Greater is He who is in me than he who is in the world. I am an overcomer by the blood of the Lamb and the word of my testimony. I can do all things through Christ who strengthens me." There is so much good Word that you can put on the situation. Change the atmosphere by playing worship music or even warfare music. For example, play the song entitled "This Means War." You may have to get up, open the windows and usher that unclean spirit out, remembering and declaring that, "I submit myself to God, I resist you, unclean spirit of __________ and you must flee."

Don't stay so focused on the unclean spirit, but begin to praise and worship God and declare who He is. As you call out His resume—Jehovah Jireh, Deliverer, Redeemer, Jehovah Rohi, the Good Shepherd, El Elyon, Lion of the Tribe of Judah, God of the Armies of Israel, Jehovah Shalom, El Hanora, Prince of Peace, and so many more, He hears you and will show up. Remember, the whole point of this is to invoke His presence so that the unclean spirit will not want to stay, nor be able to! At the name of Jesus, demons flee! We are more than conquerors through Him who loved us!

Knock, knock.

"Oh, let me see who's at the door. Sorry, you're a stranger and the voice of a stranger, I do not know you and do not follow you. I will not let you in because the peace of God, which passes all understanding, is keeping my heart and mind through Christ Jesus."

Takeaway Nugget: Discern the people, places and things to which you expose yourself.

Foundational Scripture: *Be very careful, then, how you live – not as unwise but as wise, making the most of every opportunity, because the days are evil.*
–Ephesians 5:15-16 (NIV)

Week 21

Fitting Room

I went to a concert one summer for one of my favorite male pop singers. It was a VIP event complete with free, up-close parking; a special VIP entrance and a fabulous, elaborate food spread. It was a beautiful day and I invited (though they might say "coerced") three very close friends to go with me. The singer is a classically trained pop singer with a beautiful tenor, sometimes baritone voice, known probably for melodious ballads that some people would call "opera-like." Anyway, during his opening—you know, the monologue they do before they sing a song and in-between each one—he talked about his travel tour, the various cities and just general comments that they make to connect with the audience. At one point he swore and even made some off-color, crude, somewhat indecent, dirty joke remarks. I was shocked.

To my knowledge, he had never presented or marketed himself that way, and I would not have expected that from him. He normally would have been billed as someone wholesome and very down-to-earth. What I noticed about the comments and his demeanor, though, is that it was not natural for him. He seemed uncomfortable. Seemed like he was struggling with it, so it did not come across with ease. It wasn't him and you could see, sense and feel that each time he did it. In essence, *"it didn't fit."*

As a young woman, sometimes as I was leaving the house, my father would stop me in my tracks.

"Are you going out like that?" My father asked. I looked at him, clearly puzzled by the question.

"Yeah. Why?"

"You can't go out like that; you represent me."

I never understood that at the time, but as I got older, I came to know what he meant. My father was known in certain community circles, especially within the school system and he felt that I was a reflection of him. Being a Christian, I have come to understand how he felt and what he meant. Jesus expects us to represent Him.

> *Now then we are ambassadors for Christ, as though God did beseech you by us…*
> –2 Corinthians 5:20a

Ephesians 5:1 says,

> *Be ye therefore followers of God, as dear children.*

We are to look like Christ, act like Christ and think like Christ.

The Bible says that we are ambassadors of Christ. *An ambassador* is defined as a person who acts as a representative or promoter of a specified activity. We represent who Jesus is. When people look at us, they should see Jesus. No student is greater than His teacher. Jesus said to Phillip, His disciple,

> *"If you had known Me, you would have known My Father also; and from now on you know Him and have seen Him." Philip said to Him, "Lord, show us the Father, and it is sufficient for us." Jesus said to him, "Have I been with you so long, and yet you have not known Me, Philip? He who has seen Me has seen the Father; so how can you say, 'Show us the Father'?"*
>
> –John 14:7-9 (NKJV)

If Jesus is our Father, then we should look like Him. We must constantly endeavor to put on the Christ-like nature.

> *Therefore, as the elect of God, holy and beloved, put on tender mercies, kindness, humility, meekness, longsuffering; bearing with one another, and forgiving one another, if anyone has a complaint against another; even as Christ forgave you, so you also must do. But above all these things put on love, which is the bond of perfection.*
>
> –Colossians 3:12-14 (NKJV)

When we swear, are unforgiving, speak sharply, exaggerate, are rebellious, manipulative, lie, are filled with jealousy, engage in road rage, are self-centered, rude, impatient, justify and reason out our behavior, and so on, those things do not fit who we are in Christ. We have been changed. We have a new nature, given to us by the shed blood of Jesus. Everything about us should be transformed by the renewing of our mind. We are expected to be new creatures.

> *"Therefore, if any man be in Christ, he is a new creature: old things are passed away; behold, all things are become new."*
> –2 Corinthians 5:17

Our bitterness, anger, thoughts of revenge, cheating, lying, sexual sin, sour-faced looks, operating in fear, vulgar speech and so on—all of these things do not fit the Christian lifestyle. We should become very uncomfortable whenever we try to act like that old man.

The prompting of the Holy Spirit should be convicting us and tugging at us to remind us that this behavior no longer fits. Jesus tells us that He is making us over anew. We are in the process of being

> *"...changed into the same image from glory to glory, even as by the Spirit of the Lord."*
> –2 Corinthians 3:18b

These ungodly characteristics just do not fit who we are.

> *But fornication and all uncleanness or covetousness, let it not even be named among you, as is fitting for saints; neither filthiness, nor foolish talking, nor coarse jesting, which are not fitting, but rather giving of thanks."*
> –Ephesians 5:3-4 (NKJV)

At the concert, as I watched this pop star struggle with his off-color remarks, I was saddened because I could see his discomfort as he tried to connect with the audience by being someone he was not. The reality of it all is that we would have been just fine if he had just been himself. Ironically, his audiences are made up of people who couldn't care less about those kinds of remarks. His appeal was to a gentler, more wholesome, more sedate audience, especially since his music was sometimes branded as classical pop. We just wanted to hear him sing! However, the entertainment industry consistently seeks to alter performers' images to make them grittier, edgier, and more offbeat.

Imagine how grieved our Father is when we try to be something we are not, or something we have not been called to be. He never expects us to alter our behavior to "fit" in with the popular culture or go along with the sway of the world. We are to be authentically who we were created to be. There is nothing sadder than watching a person trying to be something they are not, especially when you can see their discomfort in doing so. It's difficult to do because it's not natural. It takes more energy and concentration to do that, and those with spiritual discernment can see that's not who you really are.

Think about it in the natural. You see an item of clothing that you really like. You take it into the dressing room and try it on. You have to squeeze into it slightly. When it's finally in place, so to speak, you look in the mirror and see that it's too tight. It rides up in places it shouldn't, and because you really want it, you start justifying in your mind that it doesn't really "look that bad," and "if I pull it down or tug it this way, it's actually kind of cute." The bottom line is, "It just doesn't fit!" No matter how you tug, smooth out the wrinkles or try to cover it with a jacket - *it doesn't fit*! The same is true when we try to clothe ourselves in a character that is not Christlike.

So, if you're acting in a way that is "out of character," why try to fool others when they can see that you're faking it? Just be genuine, be real—be who God created *you* to be. We do it all the time; we try to get people to think we are one way when we really are not. We wear ourselves out covering and hiding so that no one knows what we are really like. If we are covering negative traits (meanness, greed, selfishness, laziness, for example; you fill in the blank), we might as well allow those traits to surface. Let them be exposed so we can get free! The sooner we confess to the way we really are (which others can see anyway), the sooner our deliverance will come!

Now, getting back to the original point. We must seek the Lord about our current character so that we can cry out to God and ask Him to reveal the fruit that He still needs to work in us. The Bible says,

> *"But put ye on the Lord Jesus Christ, and make not provision for the flesh, to fulfil the lusts thereof.*
>
> –Romans 13:14

We want to continually strip off the old garments that do not fit and put on or clothe ourselves with the personality and characteristics of Christ. Read the following passages of Scripture that speak to how we are to be dressed.

> *I will greatly rejoice in the LORD, my soul shall be joyful in my God; for he hath clothed me with the garments of salvation, he hath covered me with the robe of righteousness, as a bridegroom decketh himself with ornaments, and as a bride adorneth herself with her jewels.*
> –Isaiah 61:10

> *Likewise, ye younger, submit yourselves unto the elder. Yea, all of you be subject one to another, and be clothed with humility: for God resisteth the proud, and giveth grace to the humble.*
> –1 Peter 5:5

> *Wherefore take unto you the whole armor of God, that ye may be able to withstand in the evil day, and having done all, to stand. Stand therefore, having your loins girt about with truth, and having on the breastplate of righteousness; And your feet shod with the preparation of the gospel of peace; Above all, taking the shield of faith, wherewith ye shall be able to quench all the fiery darts of the wicked. And take the helmet of salvation, and the sword of the Spirit, which is the word of God:*
> –Ephesians 6:13-17

> *And that ye put on the new man, which after God is created in righteousness and true holiness.*
>
> –Ephesians 4:24

God is telling us how to be clothed. Reading about this new clothing was all very interesting, and I wish I had had more time to study it in greater depth. I encourage you to go deeper with it if this is of interest to you. Review the Scriptures that were given out and read about the spiritual wardrobe. I skimmed some good commentaries from notable scholars on this in Bible Hub, an online Bible study tool. I think we can both learn a lot from a study on this topic.

We are to wear the character of Christ. Summed up, when you head out in the morning, you should be wearing the whole armor of God and be nourished with the fruit of the Spirit, which is love, joy, peace, patience, kindness, goodness, faithfulness, gentleness and self-control. As a Christian, any other garments that you have on just don't fit. It's time to donate those garments to the Salvation Army! Get out your Discover card and go shopping for some new robes of righteousness!

Takeaway Nugget: Those old graveclothes no longer fit!

Foundational Scripture: *You were taught, with regard to your former way of life, to put off your old self, which is being corrupted by its deceitful desires; to be made new in the attitude of your minds; and to put on the new self, created to be like God in true righteousness and holiness.*

–Ephesians 4:22-24 (NIV)

Week 22

Purpose. What's Yours?

Purpose (noun): the reason for which something is done or created or for which something exists.

> *O LORD, You have searched me and known me. You know my sitting down and my rising up; You understand my thought afar off. You comprehend my path and my lying down, And are acquainted with all my ways.*
> –Psalm 139:1-3 (NKJV)

> *Your eyes saw my substance, being yet unformed. And in Your book they all were written, The days fashioned for me, When as yet there were none of them.*
> –Psalm 139:16 (NKJV)

Before you were even born, before God even created the world and brought everything into existence, He knew you. Now, that's a selah moment. Selah is a word frequently found in the Book of Psalms. It's also in Habakkuk 3:9 and Habakkuk 3:13—about seventy-four times total in Scripture. Its meaning is doubtful and unknown, but some interpret it as meaning "silence" or "pause." So really, let's think about that. Before anything was created, when the universe was void—nothingness, God knew *you*. He knew all about you—what you were going to look like, what you were going to experience as a child, the pain that you would endure throughout your lifetime, and yes, more importantly, *your purpose*. God doesn't just create something for no reason. He always has a plan and purpose for everything.

Bees perform a task vital to the survival of agriculture: pollination. In fact, one-third of our global food supply is pollinated by bees. Simply put, bees keep plants and crops alive. Without bees, humans wouldn't have very much to eat. A bridge is a structure built to span physical obstacles without closing the way underneath, such as a body of water, valley, or road, for the purpose of providing passage over the obstacle. The human body's appendix is now thought to act as a reservoir for "good bacteria." These bacteria contribute to keeping the gut healthy and support your recovery from infections. Studies' findings contradict a commonly held belief that the appendix has no function. And although one can live without an appendix, think about it: God doesn't create something that has no purpose.

Even those things that seem to be unimportant have a purpose. Like eyebrows, for example. Their main function is to prevent sweat, water, and other debris from entering the eye socket. However, eyebrows are also important to human communication and facial expression. Everything that God creates has a purpose. Simply put, *you have a purpose*!

Because God values humans far above objects and animals, the Bible says,

> *"Behold the fowls of the air: for they sow not, neither do they reap, nor gather into barns; yet your heavenly Father feedeth them. Are ye not much better than they?"*
> –Matthew 6:26

I love how the Bible tells us that God is so personal and so intimate in that He cherishes us individually. One of my favorite passages is,

> *What do you think? If a man has a hundred sheep, and one of them goes astray, does he not leave the ninety-nine and go to the mountains to seek the one that is straying? And if he should find it, assuredly, I say to you, he rejoices more over that sheep than over the ninety-nine that did not go astray."* –Matthew 18:12-13 (NKJV)

That is just how precious we are individually to God. He is El Roi—"the God who sees me"! He knows and sees you. You are not insignificant; you have a purpose!

We need to seek God for our purpose. First, we must simply ask Him and then listen. Be in tune and communicate with Him about it. Think about your gifts and talents and how He might want you to use them. Some of you are good with words and enjoy writing. God may be calling you to write devotionals. Some of you can sew and are extremely creative. I think of one of the sisters in my church and how she seeks the Lord when He gives her an idea. She creates such beauty in things like banners that it inspires us to worship God with our whole heart and being!

Maybe you have great administrative skills. You can organize and implement plans of action. Perhaps, you are being groomed to be a leader in the church or a church administrator. Perhaps you can cook or know all about culinary arts. Maybe God is calling you to start a food pantry or serve meals at the church. Maybe you are a really good listener and can understand how people feel; you've been gifted with empathy. God could be calling you to minister to people as a counselor. Only God knows those plans He has for you; it's up to you to discover them.

God is not trying to withhold this information from you. He wants you to know your purpose. He says in Jeremiah 33:3,

> *"Call unto me, and I will answer thee, and show thee great and mighty things, which thou knowest not."*

I believe God wants you to know your purpose so you can get busy for Him to use you! Trust me, no matter what your purpose is, it is a blessing to the body of Christ and the kingdom of God! To find it, though, you must spend time with the Lord. You've got to read the Word, sit quietly with Him and listen. He will begin to reveal to you why He created you, especially as you continue to walk in righteousness. You will see little glimpses of your past and why you used to do things the way you did.

All of these things are leading to your purpose. As a child and even as an adult, I loved surveys, quizzes, and making lists. I even once hoped I would get the long form for the census; when I did, I was delighted! Little did I know that these were indications of the purpose of my administrative skills.

> *But as for you, you meant evil against me; but God meant it for good, to bring it about as it is this day, to save many people alive.*
> —Genesis 50:20 (NKJV)

That was Joseph's prayer and look how that story turned out. He ended up being a second-in-command leader and saved a whole nation of people, including his family, from famine. Your purpose—no matter how great or small, it's all great in God's eyes—is calling out to you to discover it! Our world needs your purpose. Find out what it is. Say to God, "Show me, Lord, who I am. Reveal to me my purpose." I guarantee you, if you begin to cry out to the Lord like that, He will answer you. Purpose: the reason for which something is done or created or for which something exists. What's yours?

Takeaway Nugget: Even a spoon has a specific purpose. Think of how difficult it would be to eat broth with a fork. God created you for a specific purpose. You are here for a reason and you matter.

Foundational Scripture: *Like an open book, you watched me grow from conception to birth; all the stages of my life were spread out before you, the days of my life all prepared before I'd even lived one day.*

–Psalm 139:15-16 (The Message)

Week 23

No Returns, Uneven Exchanges Only

You've purchased something without any intention of bringing it back, so there was no need to ask about the return policy. Then, you find out after all that you want to return it. You take it back and there's nothing like hearing the words, "No returns; even exchanges only."

Having experienced the greater side of life through salvation, I can tell you without hesitation that I do not want to return my new life for the old one. I am going to keep the "purchase" that Jesus made for me and have no intention of taking my old life back! I know that I have other witnesses who would truly say and believe this passage:

> *Therefore if any man be in Christ, he is a new creature: old things are passed away; behold, all things are become new.*
> –2 Corinthians 5:17

There's nothing to go back to, nothing to return to in my old life. I don't miss it, and truthfully, life in the kingdom of God is far greater than anything my old life could ever have offered. The old life was death; the new life is just that—*life*, and that more abundantly!

In one of my pastor's sermons, she taught about how Jesus became the sacrificial lamb who took away the sins of the world. He made the ultimate sacrifice with His body. And now, because of what He did on the cross, we get to make an exchange through Jesus. We exchange our stuff and take what God has to become more like Jesus. How easy is that?

In manmade organizations, when you're trying to join, you have to go through all these hoops: swear by this; can't do this, can't do that and have to prove yourself worthy. But with Jesus, you don't have to go through any of those kinds of changes. All you have to do is "believe in the One who was sent." All you have to do is say, "Yes!" What an awesome God we serve! And as I often say, "Who does that?" Only our precious Lord and Savior.

So, we have the privilege and the benefit of making an exchange, but check this out: we don't make an even exchange. We get to make something even greater: an *un*even exchange! Jesus says, "*Give me your mess and take my holiness; Give me your mess and take my blessings; Give me your fears and take my peace; Give me your lack and take my abundance. Give me your weakness and take my strength.*" Here are some others, further explained with supporting Scripture:

- Give me your doubts and take my assurance and re-assurance.

  Fear not, for I am with you; Be not dismayed, for I am your God. I will strengthen you, Yes, I will help you, I will uphold you with My righteous right hand.

  –Isaiah 41:10 (NKJV)

- Give me your grief and take my comfort.

  Blessed are those who mourn, for they shall be comforted.

  –Matthew 5:4 (NIV)

  Thou hast turned for me my mourning into dancing: thou hast put off my sackcloth, and girded me with gladness;"

  –Psalm 30:11

- Give me your past and I will give you your future.

  For I know the plans I have for you," declares the Lord, "plans to prosper you and not to harm you, plans to give you hope and a future."

  –Jeremiah 29:11 (NIV)

- Give me your income or at least 10% of it, and I will give you abundant, over-the-top ROI's (Return on Investment). ROI measures the amount of return on an investment relative to the investment's cost. But with this investment, the cost is immeasurable, for it was the shed blood of Jesus. The cost was the death of God's only beloved Son. And because Jesus paid that price for us, God, who loves us unconditionally, is more than willing to give us a return that blesses us abundantly materially, but more importantly, spiritually: freedom from sin, peace of mind, righteousness, health, wisdom, acceptance, peace, joy, everlasting love, fulfillment, purpose, security in Him and eternal life both now and later.

  "Bring the whole tithe into the storehouse, that there may be food in my house. Test me in this," says the Lord Almighty, "and see if I will not

throw open the floodgates of heaven and pour out so much blessing that there will not be room enough to store it.
–Malachi 3:10 (NIV)

- Give me your thirst and take My living water.

  Whosoever drinketh of this water shall thirst again: But whosoever drinketh of the water that I shall give him shall never thirst; but the water that I shall give him shall be in him a well of water springing up into everlasting life.
  –John 4:13b-14

  Ask the woman at the well. She believed and received the gift of salvation. She made the exchange that day. She gave Jesus her questionable, shameful past and took on His offer of grace, forgiveness and a new reputation as a daughter of the Most High God! She simply said yes, and then she ran and told everyone about the gift she had just received.

  And many of the Samaritans of that city believed on him for the saying of the woman, which testified, He told me all that ever I did.
  –John 4:39

- Give me your depression and heaviness, and take my light, joy and peace.

  "Take my yoke upon you, and learn of me; for I am meek and lowly in heart: and ye shall find rest unto your souls. For my yoke is easy, and my burden is light."
  –Matthew 11:29-30

Jesus offers all of the above and so, so much more. All you have to do is say yes and have a desire to be set free, to be truly loved, cared for and to know the Truth that frees you. You'll know a love that doesn't box you in. There is no need to prove who you are, to be accepted by mankind or a need to pass man's qualifications. No stress, no yokes, no burdens. Just breathe, lie back and accept His peace, His power and His rest!

And while that last paragraph may sound like an invitation to salvation, make no mistake about it: it is. Remember, salvation is ongoing. Salvation doesn't end just because you said "Yes" and now all your problems are over. No. The work begins the moment after that. And the best part is you don't have to do the work. You don't have to work to change yourself—you can't anyway. Only the power of the Holy Spirit can do that.

Because Jesus is so loving, He does the work for you. All you have to do is keep saying yes, keep confessing, keep forgiving, keep praising Him, keep reading, believing and obeying the Word of God. Watch Him transform you.

> *For it is God which worketh in you both to will and to do of his good pleasure.*
> —Philippians 2:13

What an awesome deal that is! You won't find a better offer anywhere else! This offer never expires; you can renew it at any time (the cost does go up each time, but it's worth it—it's called "spiritual growth"). And the offer comes with a lifetime warranty with no depreciation in value of the product. It's not too late; you can sign up today!

And for those of us who are already saved and have been walking with the Lord for a little while, our salvation is a daily event. We have brand new mercies every morning. We have an opportunity to live a kingdom life filled with promise, benefits, purpose, and a new way of thinking and interacting. It's a choice; just say yes to Jesus every time. Give Him whatever you've been holding on to. Relax your grip on it and open your hand so that He can give you the best uneven exchange you could never imagine! *Call now; operators are standing by*!

Takeaway Nugget: Whatever it is that's plaguing you, give it to God. Jesus has already made the exchange for it.

Foundational Scripture: *For he hath made him to be sin for us, who knew no sin; that we might be made the righteousness of God in him.*
–2 Corinthians 5:21

Week 24

Giving Your Inward Parts an Out Loud Voice

Reality court TV shows have always fascinated me, but there were very few that I watched. There was one show featuring a female judge who I liked because she was fair and honest without being sensational or mean. She's a smart cookie and I liked how she listened to discern who was being truthful and who wasn't, which is, of course, part of her training.

What fascinated me most, though, was the litigants' reactions. No matter how wrong they were and how much evidence was presented against them, sometimes, by their own words, they still believed they were right. After the verdict was issued, they were still arguing their case during the brief interview portion, even though they lost. They attempted to justify why they were right. I am amazed at the utter arrogance and resilience they showed despite having been proven wrong or told so.

The Bible says,

> *Behold, thou desirest truth in the inward parts: and in the hidden part thou shalt make me to know wisdom.*
>
> −Psalm 51:6

It's doubtful that many of those litigants are believers; we see and hear so much ugliness, immaturity, spite and covering in their behavior and words. Their inward parts are harboring an overabundance of anger, hostility, pride, unforgiveness, hatred, vengeance, insecurity, bitterness, meanness, defensiveness and the list goes on. While probably about five percent of the cases had some validity, the other 95% of what they were suing over were petty and trivial, stemming from a lack of understanding of the other person's heart and an unwillingness to simply say, "I am wrong."

As we live in a fallen, carnal world, this is not surprising to witness, but it is so sad to watch and further emphasizes just how much we need Jesus. Of course, we need Jesus. For every problem, the answer is Jesus. As I watched this show, which was only a very minor commentary on our world today, I couldn't help but feel grief in my heart, with a tear in my spiritual eye, truly sympathizing with the heart of our Lord and how saddened He must be as He looks upon the hearts of people.

In the particular case that I was watching, a daughter was suing her mother over an unpaid cell phone bill. There was a lot of discussion on both sides. As the judge tried to determine how she was going to rule, the main point she tried to get them to hear was the loss of a relationship between a mother and daughter. She spoke about how trivial the case was and that it would pass away, but their relationship and the impact it was having on the seven-year-old child caught between them are the things that really mattered and will not be forgotten.

As they left the courtroom, both women were interviewed separately. Unfortunately, this is what each had to say:

The mother: "I no longer have a daughter; I am done."

The daughter: "There can be no relationship; she has used me all my life and if she were on fire and I had to spit on her to put it out, I would walk away."

As I heard their words, I was shocked, grieved and saddened to hear of such deep-seated hatred between two human beings, let alone a mother and a daughter. The "I'm not a therapist, but play one on TV" in me is so fascinated by relationships and by how people get to that point. I would really like to know what brought them to that point in life. And while I believe these women were unbelievers, we in the body of Christ are not that much different. If only there was a way to bring healing and reconciliation. Oh, wait; there is. His name is Jesus!

Suffice it to say, that without Jesus, there can be no true forgiveness and repair of this type of breach. He alone brings about lasting and pure reconciliation through knowledge, understanding and application of His Word. There is no other way. With man, that would be impossible; but with God, all things are possible. The supernatural anointing and the power of the blood of Jesus can mend any broken relationship, whether it's a deep-seated one like this or some other minor offense.

So, where do we start? We start in the inward parts. We have to examine our hearts and cry out constantly to God to ask Him to reveal what is going on inside of us. And sometimes, we have to do that out loud. Read the following Scripture, which reflects what's going on inside of us and how it gets expressed:

> *A good man out of the good treasure of his heart bringeth forth that which is good; and an evil man out of the evil treasure of his heart bringeth forth that which is evil: for of the abundance of the heart his mouth speaketh.*
>
> –Luke 6:45

We should constantly be aware of what is going on in our hearts.

We must guard our hearts. Whatever is going on inside determines our thoughts. What we meditate upon directs our actions and behavior. For example, let's say that I am angry about a comment my husband made just before I left home that was not resolved. By now, that anger is stirring around in my heart while I'm driving. Now, I am thinking about it—even rehearsing what was said and meditating upon what I am going to say later. For one thing, I am distracted, but let someone cut me off and my reaction could easily turn into road rage—yelling at the car or even speaking profanities. Certainly not my finest hour and definitely not representing the Christ who lives in me.

I see people today as little boiling pots. Something is always brewing and bubbling inside of us. When the heat is turned up high, if the lid isn't removed in time, it can fly off and could cause harm to whoever is in its path. This is why it's so important to be in tune with what's going on inside of us. I mentioned crying out to the Lord and asking Him, "What's going on with me?" It doesn't even have to be anger; it could be any number of things: depression, grief, disappointment, dissatisfaction, lust, confusion—the list is endless.

When we are in tune to our emotions and our thoughts, we can talk with the Lord about them. One of our Great I AM's names is Wonderful Counselor. No appointment is necessary and just getting His perspective on what is going on with us is priceless. This can open the door to great revelation and insight about ourselves. And then, sometimes even without asking, He will give us an appropriate Scripture to meditate upon to transform us. That's how we renew the mind. As our mind is renewed, it can tell our body what to do and our behavior can change! This is good news! What a great process He has given us.

So, let's go back to where we started. We must be truthful with the inward parts. We need to first be honest with ourselves before God and in our relationships with others. And sometimes we need to do it with an out loud voice.

Maybe today, it's time to just say these kinds of things to God in all honesty and sincerity:

- I'm angry
- I'm dissatisfied with my life; it hasn't turned out the way I wanted it to
- I'm hurting
- My parents weren't there for me; my mother wasn't who I needed her to be
- My father left and that hurts; he has been absent all my life
- I am obsessed with food, shopping, sex, sports, money and material things, [fill in the blank], and I am using those things as substitutes to fulfill me
- I am a slob, a user; I'm prejudiced, I'm [fill in the blank]

When you express these kinds of things out loud to God, several things can and do happen. For one, you get a breakthrough. God hears you and is moved to help you. Remember, He draws near to those of a broken spirit and a contrite heart. The door opens for Him to come in, where before it was nailed shut by your dishonesty and unwillingness to speak out on some things. Your confession disarms the enemy because you exposed your issue and now, there's nothing the enemy can do with it. He likes to work undercover and in secret. Well, since you've exposed it, the enemy has nothing to work with. And you've just put him on notice: "Yeah, I've confessed this and I don't want to stay the way I am. I've cried out to God and He heard me. He is already on the way to help; so you're fired!"

Maybe today, it's time, in all honesty and sincerity, to just say these kinds of things to someone in your life:

- I'm sorry; please forgive me
- I was wrong
- It was not my intention to hurt you; I am sorry
- We haven't spoken in so long and I just wanted to call to tell you that I miss our friendship; I miss the relationship we had
- Can we talk?

These are words of healing. They may not be easy to say—no one said it would be easy- but God just expects us to do it. Then, His grace can kick in and help to bring reconciliation and restoration. That is the whole message of the cross and His greatest desire. We keep hearing it over and over.

And thou shalt love the Lord thy God with all thy heart, and with all thy soul, and with all thy mind, and with all thy strength: this is the first commandment. And the second is like, namely this, Thou shalt love thy neighbor as thyself. There is none other commandment greater than these.
–Mark 12:30-31

Today is always a great day to start. Let's begin with truth in the inward parts so that in the hidden part, God shall make us to know wisdom. And once you have some wisdom about what is going on inside, ask the Holy Spirit to help you speak it out loud immediately to Him in prayer and, if need be, to the others He places on your heart, but only in His timing as directed by Him.

Takeaway Nugget: Express to God your true feelings. He already knows them, but He's waiting for you to open your mouth and cry out so that He can help you.

Foundational Scripture: *For there is not a word on my tongue, But behold, O LORD, You know it altogether.*
–Psalm 139:4 (NKJV)

Week 25

Still He Speaks From Eternity

God has much to say to us. He is the all-wise and sovereign God. Because of our finite humanity, as well as our fallenness, it is imperative for us to listen carefully.

We are not who we are at any given moment in our lives. Who we are is the sum total of our lives and all its experiences. No person is just any one thing, good or bad. We are different things at various stages in our journey, and those make up the seasons of our life. Across every season, God is there, orchestrating each moment and developing our character. In all those times, this is what He says:

- When you are weak, I AM says:

  My grace is sufficient for thee: for my strength is made perfect in weakness.

  –2 Corinthians 12:9a
- When you are sick or going through a long period of illness, I AM says:

  He sent his word, and healed them, and delivered them from their destructions.

  –Psalm 107:20

  Beloved, I wish above all things that thou mayest prosper and be in health, even as thy soul prospereth.

  –3 John 1:2

- When you experience times of loneliness, short or extended, I AM says:

  I will never leave thee, nor forsake thee.

  –Hebrews 13:5b

  Lo, I am with you always, even unto the end of the world. Amen.

  –Matthew 28:20b

- When you're down on yourself, or when you feel like you just can't get it together, I AM says:

  For if our heart condemns us, God is greater than our heart, and knoweth all things.

  –1 John 3:20

  Greater is he that is in you, than he that is in the world.

  –1 John 4:4b

- When you feel stuck—nothing good is happening, nothing bad is happening, I AM says:

  And let us not be weary in well doing: for in due season we shall reap, if we faint not.

  –Galatians 6:9

- When you are misunderstood and feel that no one understands you, David wrote that, I AM says:

  O LORD, thou hast searched me, and known me. Thou knowest my downsitting and mine uprising, thou understandest my thought afar off. Thou compassest my path and my lying down, and art acquainted with all my ways. For there is not a word in my tongue, but, lo, O LORD, thou knowest it altogether.

  –Psalm 139:1-4

- When you are feeling on top of the world and think you've got it going on, and you begin to show it in your speech and actions, I AM says:

  Not to think of himself more highly than he ought to think; but to think soberly…

  –Romans 12:3b

  For without me ye can do nothing.

  –John 15:5b

  Understand that I am he: before me there was no God formed, neither shall there be after me. I, even I, am the LORD; and beside Me there is no savior.

  –Isaiah 43:10b-11

- When you have lost all hope, I AM says:

  Now the God of hope fill you with all joy and peace in believing, that ye may abound in hope, through the power of the Holy Ghost.

  –Romans 15:13

  And she called the name of the LORD that spake unto her, Thou God seest me:

  –Genesis 16:13a

  Can a woman forget her sucking child, that she should not have compassion on the son of her womb? Yea, they may forget, yet I will not forget thee.

  –Isaiah 49:15

No matter what season of life you are in, no matter the challenges or the joys, for better or for worse, for richer or for poorer, in sickness and in health, God sees you. God hears you and He still speaks from eternity!

Takeaway Nugget: Speak to me, Lord. I am listening for Your voice.

Foundational Scripture: *But the word of the Lord endureth forever.*
–1 Peter 1:25a

Week 26

Spiritually Healthy

There are several things we must do to remain spiritually healthy. We must daily put on the armor of God to be both offensively and defensively ready and positioned against the enemy's attacks. We must get dressed daily, putting on the belt of truth, the helmet of salvation, the breastplate of righteousness, the shoes fitted with the readiness of the gospel of peace, the shield of faith, with which we can extinguish all the flaming arrows of the evil one, and most importantly, the sword of the Spirit, which is the Word of God.

Other things we must do to maintain spiritual health include, of course, confessing and repenting of our sin, praising and worshiping, daily reading and studying the Word, quickly forgiving all offenses, great or small, tithing, and assembling together with other believers, just to name a few. We also need to make sure that we get the recommended daily allowance (RDA) of our vitamins. The recommended daily allowance is the amount of a vitamin or mineral you need to keep healthy and stay well-nourished.

Today, I want to review with you five important vitamins that you should take daily. They are Vitamin C, Vitamin K, Vitamin H, Vitamin G and Vitamin P. Let's look at each one individually.

Therefore, as God's chosen people, holy and dearly loved, clothe yourselves with compassion, kindness, humility, gentleness and patience.
–Colossians 3:12 (NIV)

Vitamin C - Compassion. We need to take in a daily allowance of Vitamin C (Compassion). The definition of compassion is "sympathetic pity and concern for the sufferings or misfortunes of others."

This vitamin is good for your heart. It makes it soft and tender and prevents *arteriosclerosis*, which is the hardening of your emotions, your sensitivities and your concern for others. This vitamin prevents unforgiveness and bitterness; it should be taken in large amounts daily. It wards against one of the deadliest diseases targeting Christians today, which is *selfishness*. Ten out of 10 doctors recommended this vitamin as essential to spiritual health.

I would like to interject with a brief testimony of God's very amazing, specific communication with us when we are in a personal, specific and intimate relationship with Him. One morning, I was talking to God about birthing greater compassion in me. I was expressing to Him that I guess I didn't have a very good understanding of compassion and that I genuinely wanted to become a more compassionate person. I cried out to the Lord about showing mercy and asked for greater understanding.

Later that same day, I remembered that I had been given a gift from one of my ministry sisters that I had not opened. I went to get it and opened up the wrapping paper. Inside was a small gift of a clip-on booklight for reading. It was inexpensive—possibly a dollar-store item—but I appreciated it and knew that I could use it. I flipped it over and, on the back, amidst the instructions, my eyes fell upon some writing. I stood there, frozen in amazement. My mouth was open as I read the words: "Compassion is to willingly undergo hardship for the sake of others." C'mon now! Who speaks directly to His children on the back of a dollar store booklight?! Only an amazing, supernatural, sweet, loving, personal, real and *awesome* God! When God wants to get a message to you, He can and will use just about anything! I will never forget that and it blessed me tremendously!

Vitamin K - Kindness. The quality of being friendly, generous, considerate, warm, caring and concerned.

This vitamin is taken in small doses so that you can practice little random acts of it all throughout the day. It is one of the few vitamins that you can take in excess without causing harm. Vitamin K is good for the brain because it causes you to think of ways that you can bless others, ways that you can help someone out, and it keeps the focus off yourself.

Vitamin H - Humility. The definition of humility is "a modest or low view of one's own importance; not proud or haughty; not arrogant or assertive; reflecting, expressing, or offered in a spirit of deference or submission."

Vitamin H should be taken every day, preferably first thing in the morning. This vitamin is rich in nutrients that help protect against a variety of manifestations such as pride, arrogance, and fleshly zeal. Vitamin H is good for the knees because you should be on your knees often when practicing humility. Vitamin H (Humility) is the greatest prevention of misunderstandings, which is the leading cause of unforgiveness and broken relationships.

Vitamin G - Gentleness. The quality of being kind, tender, or mild-mannered; softness of action or effect.

Vitamin G is similar in its nutrients to Vitamin K (Kindness) and should be taken in conjunction with it to achieve maximum benefits. It is often considered a supplement to Vitamin K. Vitamin G is inexpensive, widely available, and easily swallowed and digested.

Vitamin P - Patience. The capacity to accept or tolerate delay, trouble or suffering without getting angry or upset.

Vitamin P is one of the best vitamins for mature growth. It builds character and helps us to *endure discomfort without complaint*.

When taken regularly, Vitamin P has been known to prevent rash decisions, costly mistakes, unwise choices and harmful words that cannot be taken back. One cannot overdose on Vitamin P. Vitamin P is one of the most beneficial vitamins in the life of a Christian and should be taken daily as often as needed.

Takeaway Nugget: So, beloved, be sure that along with putting on your armor daily, also remember to take your vitamins to boost your spiritual immune system and enhance your Christian walk.

Foundational Scripture: *Therefore, as God's chosen people, holy and dearly loved, clothe yourselves with compassion, kindness, humility, gentleness and patience.*
–Colossians 3:12 (NIV)

Week 27

Tools for Successful Christian Growth

God gave me a formula that I would like to share with you.

TOOLS = CHANGE = HOPE

I believe that people today are losing hope. Our focus is on what we see happening around us or on the fact—not the truth—but the fact that we don't see things changing in our lives. It's the same old thing day in and day out, and that can cause people to just go through the motions or even to give up truly living. The Bible says this about lost hope:

> *"Hope deferred maketh the heart sick: but when the desire cometh, it is a tree of life."*
> –Proverbs 13:12

When we don't see things changing, we lose hope. But what needs to change most is *us*. We need to grow spiritually.

But how do we do that? Well, we need tools. We need tools to help us. A tool is simply a device that aids in accomplishing a task. There is nothing like a good tool to change things, to make something that was difficult easier to do. Let's look at some of the tools you can use as a Christian to bring about change in your spiritual walk!

- Bible. First and foremost, you need a Bible. To grow as a Christian, you have to read your Bible, with the goal of reading it every day or at least regularly. You can read a little or a lot, but you must read it if you want to see change.
- Concordance. Get a good concordance. A concordance is an alphabetical index of the main words of a book, like a Bible, that shows all the places where a particular word can be found. For example, a concordance would show you all the places where the word praise or shepherd or holy can be found in the Scriptures. Then you can go to each of those passages to get a greater understanding of a word or even a topic.
- Strong's Concordance. Strong's is a special concordance that allows you to look up words in the languages of the Bible: Hebrew (Old Testament) and Greek (New Testament). This is a fulfilling and delightful way to see the expanded meanings of words, allowing one to have a much deeper revelation of God's Word. I highly recommend doing this.
- Bible Dictionary. Just as we look up regular words that we don't know in a dictionary, there are biblical terms and words we don't always understand. A good Bible dictionary will help explain those words to provide greater understanding. A regular dictionary has those same words, and it can be very helpful to look

them up there and in the Bible dictionary. Looking up the meaning of words like redeemed, justified or righteous can really help us better understand who we are as Christians and helps us to grow.

- Get to know Jesus
    - Read the Book of John. The Book of John was written to show that Jesus of Nazareth was Christ, the Son of God, and that believers in Him might have eternal life.
    - Study God's names, for example, [El Elyon (Most High God), El Emet (God of Truth), Jehovah Jireh (Provider), Jehovah Rapha (Healer)]. Studying His names will help you recognize when He shows up in your life as that name, which gives you a personal testimony, increases your faith, and helps you to know which name to call on when you have a need.
    - Study Jesus' character, which is so closely tied to His names. Study and learn about Him as omnipotent, transcendent, eternal, immutable and so many more. As you learn about who He is in the deeper meaning of these words, you will become more intimately acquainted with Him and your relationship will grow.

Remember, these are tools, and TOOLS = CHANGE = HOPE.

- Pray/Prayer. Prayer draws you closer to God. It also takes your focus off yourself and your problems. Pray for others. You'll never run short of things to pray about. Purchase some good prayer books to help you with your prayers. Ask a trusted friend or pastor to recommend some.

- Devotionals. A devotional provides readings for each day of the year or even shorter time frames (e.g., 31 days, 40 days). They all vary, and there is no requirement for the number of days. It usually has a format, purpose, and provides a time for daily prayer and meditation. The purpose of a devotional is to encourage spiritual growth. There are many, varying in style and length. You're reading through one right now. Find one that you will enjoy. A devotional helps keep you on track.
- Memorize Scripture. Use flash cards or put your favorite Scriptures on 3 X 5 index cards. This helps get the word down into your spirit so you can call on it when you need it. The Word is powerful and it works; it brings change, life and healing to your spirit and situation.
- Pray in the Spirit. If you are infilled with the Holy Spirit, you have received a prayer language. This language, which is distinct from the actual gift of tongues, is available to every believer and is used to communicate with God by the power of the Holy Spirit.

"But you, beloved, building yourselves up on your most holy faith, praying in the Holy Spirit."
–Jude 1:12

It is the language that we can and should use often to build ourselves up, to strengthen and encourage us.

- The Internet. You can use the Internet to find many great podcasts, online quizzes, online Bible studies and narratives, mostly all for free. Be discerning, though, to ensure you are reading authentic, Bible-based, Christian material. Ask the Holy Spirit for guidance.
- Make a list of songs to sing. Carry that list with you so you can sing songs to lift your spirits. Yes, you can stream music or listen to the radio, but there is something about singing the songs you like that draws you closer to God as a personal form of praise, worship and thanksgiving.
- Post things up. Tape Scriptures, affirmations, simple prayers or general words of encouragement on your mirrors or in select spots in your home as reminders to uplift you.
- Join a Bible Study.
- Get on a conference call prayer line.

The definition of insanity is "doing the same thing over and over, but expecting different results."

If we are ever going to see change—first in ourselves, and then in those around us—we must start somewhere and we must *do* something differently.

Takeaway Nugget: God has given us many tools to help us develop and grow as Christians. Use them.

Foundational Scripture: *But be ye doers of the word, and not hearers only, deceiving your own selves.*
–James 1:22

Week 28

"I'm Just Tired"

"I'm just tired."

How many times have you heard someone say that or have said it yourself? I'm just tired. But what does that really mean? There is only one occurrence of the word tired in the Bible and its meaning is not what you might traditionally associate it with. The word tired is used in 2 Kings 9:30 KJV: And when Jehu was come to Jezreel, Jezebel heard of it; and she painted her face, and tired her head, and looked out at a window. This is the only occurrence of that word in the Bible. In that verse, it comes from the Hebrew word yâtab (YAW-TAB), which has several meanings; but for the most part, it means "to make beautiful, better, right, comely, cheerful." In other words, she was primping or fixing herself up. What does this say to us about that word?

It is okay to be weary. Listen to the meaning of it here in John 4:6 in reference to Jesus.

> *Now Jacob's well was there. Jesus therefore, being wearied with his journey, sat thus on the well: and it was about the sixth hour.*

Here, the word wearied or weary in the Greek is kopiaō (KOP-EE-AH-O), and it means "to feel fatigue, to work hard, bestow labor, toil." In Webster's Dictionary, it means "having the strength much exhausted by toil or violent exertion, tired, fatigued, worn out."

What is God speaking to us here? I believe He is telling us to take the word tired out of our vocabulary altogether. Why? Because when some people say it, it means, "I'm done; I'm giving up; I can't take it anymore; I can't go on. I don't want to go on living; I'm ready to just throw in the towel." This kind of attitude and verbal expression only fuels feelings of depression, desperation, inertia, laziness, procrastination, staying stuck and stagnant and even thoughts of suicide.

Jesus was not tired; He was weary. Weary from what? From all the work He was doing, from pressing on to do the Father's will, to continue the task He had been given despite sore muscles, aching feet, hunger, lack of sleep and the need to just sit down and be refreshed.

We can be weary, but we cannot be tired. I challenge you to be on the lookout for this word in conversation. Ask God for discernment about what the person means when they use the word "tired." Some people really do mean "weary" when they say "tired;" they are talking about their physical state and that's okay. But others are indicating to you that they want to give up. They are feeling hopeless because they feel like life is beating them up (and it may be), but we all need to get into the Word of God and keep going. Everyone needs encouragement from time to time and that's okay, but there is only one way that things will change and get better. The Word. So, this is what we need to tell others and even ourselves.

Keep going; watch your conversation: replace the word tired with weary or don't speak it out at all. Instead, say what the Word says:

"I can do all things through Christ who strengthens me."

"I am more than a conqueror through Him who loves me."

"I am an overcomer by the blood of the lamb and the word of my testimony."

"I may be troubled on every side, yet not distressed; I may be perplexed, but not in despair; I may be persecuted, but not forsaken; I may be cast down, but not destroyed..."

"The LORD is my strength and my shield; my heart trusts in Him, and I am helped..."

"I press toward the mark for the prize of the high calling of God in Christ Jesus."

We need to press on. The old saying goes, "There's a blessing in the pressing." We need to get into the Word and feed on it as fuel. We need to ingest it and let it energize us. We can't give up! We must keep going. There is work for us to do. God has given each of us assignments that He wants to accomplish only through us. He has a path of destiny for every single one of us.

The Lord is telling us not to be weary in well-doing, for in due season, we will reap if we faint not. Read the following words, which mean the same as "persist." Relax and see what God is telling you to do:

Persist, continue, carry on, go on, keep on, keep going, struggle on, hammer away, be persistent, be determined, see/follow it through, keep at it, press on/ahead, not take no for an answer, be tenacious, stand your ground, stand fast, stand firm, hold on, go the distance, stay the course, plod on, stop at nothing, leave no stone unturned; soldier on, hang on, plug away, stick to your guns, stick it out.

And if you ever really feel like you can't go on, cry out to Jesus, the good Shepherd, who says to you, "My rod and My staff, they comfort you." That staff has a hook on it so that when you veer off the path, it gently reaches and stretches as far as it needs to—depending on the distance you've gone—and then it crooks around your little sheep neck and guides you tenderly and lovingly back onto the path of righteousness. It's the ancient version of today's "lane assist."

That staff will ensure that you won't go astray, that you don't crash into anything around you, and that you do not become weary. It lets you know that His eye is on the sparrow and that God is still on the throne. El Roi sees you and will not let you faint, falter, fail or fall. His right hand is holding you up. He surrounds you and will keep you on the path of your destiny. Confess, repent, trust in Jesus, change your conversation, speak only His word and watch Him

> *...giveth power to the faint; and to them that have no might he increaseth strength. Even the youths shall faint and be weary, and the young men shall utterly fall: But they that wait upon the LORD shall renew their strength; they shall mount up with wings as eagles; they shall run, and not be weary; and they shall walk, and not faint.*
>
> –Isaiah 40:29-31

Takeaway Nugget: Be discerning when you hear the word "tired" coming from your lips or from someone else's.

Foundational Scripture: *Come unto me, all ye that labor and are heavy laden, and I will give you rest.*
–Matthew 11:28

Week 29

6-Month Check Up

But be ye doers of the word, and not hearers only,
deceiving your own selves.
–James 1:22

As believers, there is a great need for change and growth every day. To grow in faith, we must be open and willing to the work of the Holy Spirit to deliver, renew, enlighten and change us. To be sure, we must depend on the Holy Spirit's work, as it is He who brings about the change in us. However, at the same time, we must be doers of the Word in order to grow, mature and elevate. But how do we measure change? First and foremost, others should see the development of character as evidenced in our displaying the fruit of the Spirit: love, joy, peace, patience, goodness, kindness, faithfulness, gentleness and self-control. However, on a practical level, we can also see change as we take inventory of our spiritual lives.

To become or stay spiritually healthy, we must keep ourselves on a regular schedule. There are certain disciplines that we must practice daily, or as a well-known pastor puts it, "The goal is daily, but try for regularly." Consistency is the key to progress and seeing change. Consistency is the key to keeping the enemy at bay and in check. This is certainly true in our natural life. If we exercise on a regular basis, we will stay in good physical shape. When we get off the schedule or stop altogether, our bones dry out, our muscles weaken and we lose strength, stamina and energy. We must keep the momentum going.

Today, we are going to take a test to see where we are. As you read these statements, check them off to keep a tally of these "disciplines" you should practice:

1. In the morning, daily or regularly, I spend some time in worship.
2. In the morning, daily or regularly, I have a time of devotion (quiet time with the Lord).
3. I have at least one Bible, in a translation (not a paraphrase or an interpretation) that I understand, that I use, meaning that I open it up and read it daily or regularly.
4. At some time during a week, I listen to and meditate upon podcasts or radio broadcasts of biblically sound, Christ-centered spiritual leaders.
5. Having been taught how, I now have access to a Strong's Concordance and have studied a passage(s) of Scripture in the Hebrew or Greek to obtain greater clarity and deeper meaning of those verses.
6. I have a set aside time to pray for others in a quiet place where I am alone with God.
7. I spend *at least* 10 minutes daily in solitude, shut off from outside interference, where I am not talking or necessarily praising and worshipping, but just sitting alone in complete stillness, focused on God. This is a time when I allow Him to speak to me or just know that He is communicating with me.

8. At some point during a week, I have spent time reviewing and meditating upon the names of God or His characteristics to get a greater understanding of who my Lord and Savior is.
9. I have times of actual study, not just reading of the Bible. I own a Bible dictionary and use it as a reference.
10. I pray in the Spirit, meaning, in my prayer language, at least five minutes daily.

    But ye, beloved, building up yourselves on your most holy faith, praying in the Holy Ghost, keep yourselves in the love of God, looking for the mercy of our Lord Jesus Christ unto eternal life.

    –Jude 20-21
11. After the morning time, I thank, praise and worship throughout the day on a daily basis.

    Rejoice evermore. Pray without ceasing. In everything give thanks: for this is the will of God in Christ Jesus concerning you.

    –1 Thessalonians 5:16-18
12. I have favorite verses written down on paper, index cards or on my phone—not just to memorize them, but to allow the reciting of them to get down into my spirit. That way, the Word will surface up, like "rivers of living water" at a time of need.
13. I read other Christian material to edify me, encourage me and increase my spiritual knowledge. I have read at least one book in the last six months.
14. I re-read the notes I take in service or Bible study and meditate upon the major points that spoke to me.

15. I am humbly asking the Holy Spirit to reveal my character to me, to reveal those faults, flaws, wounds from the past, those people I have not forgiven and the habits that keep me in bondage to myself. I take accountability for what has been revealed and cry out to the Lord to change me. I accept His correction, confess it privately and/or publicly and then make a declaration that I am giving those things over to Him as I await the manifestation of change.

Okay! Let's see how you did!

Scoring Key:

15 You're an overcomer!

10 - 14 What can man do to you?!

5 - 9 You are God's child, holy and dearly loved!

1 - 4 No weapon formed against you shall prosper!

Beloved, we are on a journey with an expected end—eternal life with our Lord and Savior, Jesus! The Bible tells us in Matthew 5:48,

> *"Be ye therefore perfect, even as your Father which is in heaven is perfect."*

The word *perfect* here means "mature." We must continue to grow, continue to study and continue to seek the Lord for change in our character so that we become more Christ-like. We want our hearts to be right and our actions to reflect that so that others will be drawn to know and follow Jesus.

We must let our light so shine before men so that they will see our good works and glorify your Father which is in heaven. The only way that we can do this is by being doers of the Word and not hearers only. We want change to be evident in us; that can only happen as we continue to practice the disciplines we have been given and follow the example that Jesus left for us in His Word. These are simply the tools He has given us. And, as we read on a previous day, tools = change = hope.

If we are to have any hope of seeing change in our lives, we must daily, or at least regularly, keep the commandments we have been given. We do our part and the Lord does the rest. He is gracious enough to have promised us that He will bring about the change in us if we humble ourselves, take up our cross daily and follow Him. What a great deal that is! We won't find a better bargain anywhere, and I, for one, want to take Him up on that opportunity! Don't you?

Takeaway Nugget: Check your spiritual odometer every six months to gauge your growth in the knowledge of the Lord.

Foundational Scripture: *But grow in grace, and in the knowledge of our Lord and Savior Jesus Christ.*
–2 Peter 3:18a

Week 30

Victory Over the Enemy

Read Exodus 17:8-13

Focus Verse: Exodus 17:12

But Moses hands were heavy; and they took a stone, and put it under him, and he sat thereon; and Aaron and Hur stayed up his hands, the one on the one side, and the other on the other side; and his hands were steady until the going down of the sun.

The Amalekites were coming against the Israelites and forced them into battle. Sometimes, our enemies come upon us suddenly and we have no choice but to fight back. We get sick, our finances change, a loved one dies, and we have an unexpected fire or major unplanned home repair. Our circumstances can change quickly, sometimes literally overnight. Oftentimes, we are not prepared; what faces us looms large and can be very discouraging. But the Lord wants us to know, remember and believe that the battle is not ours; we are not in it alone. We will always have Him; His guidance and wisdom are always available for the asking. He will never leave us or forsake us.

There is another great source of encouragement that we often do not remember and that is the covering by our brothers and sisters in Christ through intercessory prayers! When we are weak, discouraged, possibly even very sick, it is a comfort to know that others are praying for us. There are times in our lives when we don't have the strength, or even the will, to pray for ourselves or to stir ourselves up. At these times, it is a blessing to know that our friends in the Lord have our back and are praying for us; they are interceding, going before the Lord on our behalf, standing between the problem and the answer, taking our concerns to the Lord for us. What a blessing that is!

This is why intercession is so important. It is vital, actually. To *intercede* means "to act or intervene on behalf of someone in difficulty or trouble, as by pleading or petition."

When we can't pray for ourselves, an intercessor can pray for us. Jesus is, of course, our chief intercessor, and Hebrews 7:25 tells us that *"...He ever liveth to make intercession for them."* There are many people in need of prayer and sometimes, they have no one or very few people praying for them. Remember to keep others lifted up in prayer; we need each other. This is why God places certain people on our hearts. No one person can pray for all the concerns. I believe that God lays different people on each of our hearts so that everyone and every situation is covered, including our own needs. As we pray for others, our needs are taken care of, or at the very least, it takes our minds off our own difficulties. Hopefully, it's making us more grateful for what we have. We often hear that "if we take care of God's business, He will take care of ours!"

When I think of all the people on prayer lists, especially those who are sick, who are dealing with very complex and challenging illnesses, the importance of praying for one another is now greater than ever. Pray for others. Pray, first and foremost, for their salvation and a personal relationship with the Lord Jesus Christ. Then pray for them to seek God for the root of their illness and the wisdom to treat it. We need each other; we need to have each other's backs to fight these common enemies.

One of the best ways we can help each other is by holding up each other's arms when those arms become too heavy. Aaron and Hur stayed up Moses' arms. When Moses' arms were up, Joshua and the Israelites prevailed. God is calling us today to be an Aaron and a Hur to stand in the gap for others in prayer and intercession, to make up the hedge and usher in the triumphant victory in the lives of others over their already defeated foes!

Takeaway Nugget: Pray for others.

Foundational Scripture: *Praying always with all prayer and supplication in the Spirit, and watching thereunto with all perseverance and supplication for all saints;*
–Ephesians 6:18

Week 31

Follow the Leader

Subtitle: Integrity Check

"As the LORD commanded Moses, so the children of Israel did, and they divided the land."
–Joshua 14:5

Integrity -
- the quality of being honest and having strong moral principles; moral uprightness.
- the quality or state of being complete or undivided; completeness
- the state of being whole and undivided
- internal consistency or lack of corruption

Rule -
- a principle or regulation governing conduct, action or procedure
- a prescribed guide for conduct or action;
- a regulating principle

Policy -
- prudence or wisdom in the management of one's affairs

We sometimes hear people say, "Do your own thing" or "If it feels good, do it." These statements mean to live, act, or behave in the way you want, without paying attention to convention or depending on other people.

One morning, I was walking into the building with a co-worker. This was our conversation:

Me: We're not supposed to enter from the front. They want us to go around the back.

Her: I don't follow rules like that.

Me: I'm a rule follower.

Her: I am, too—when they make sense.

Me: I don't make that determination.

Her: It just doesn't make sense to go around when we're not open yet and there's nobody in the lobby.

Me: They must have their reasons.

By this time, I had followed my co-worker right through the front door. And there was other conversation between us.

"I'm sorry I made you break the rule," my co-worker said.

"You don't have to apologize to me; I made the decision to follow," I responded.

God gave us commands and principles to live by for many reasons:

- To determine our level of faithfulness and our commitment to follow Him
- To see if we will be obedient
- To keep us humble and from arrogantly "doing our own thing."
- For our protection and safety

- To maintain order and to establish standards

Rules are put into place for a reason. We don't always understand them, and we certainly don't always agree with them, but a higher authority has established them with a purpose in mind. As God's chosen people, we are called to be obedient, to set an example of moral excellence and not allow others to sway us into doing the wrong thing just because it's convenient and because everyone else is doing it.

The world is going to do what it does, but as Christians, we are called to a higher standard. We are called to be righteous, blameless, honest, and noble. We're to act with integrity, honor, justice and moral excellence. That's why we are called a "peculiar" people. We are to be set apart, honoring the Lord in our conduct.

As I think back on the experience with my co-worker, I feel sad. I had an overwhelming sense of sadness for our world and man's arrogance in thinking that we can just do what we want and that it doesn't matter. And even more so, that we take it so lightly. It's a blatant disregard and disrespect for authority; simply put, it is sin. This is how our society has gotten to the place we are in today—a society with no standards and no conscience.

We need to pray for salvation, for souls to be saved, so that hearts can be changed and kingdom principles can be embraced. As our way of thinking aligns with God's thoughts, hopefully our actions will follow; God will be glorified and the world will function as it was originally intended.

> *"When the righteous are in authority, the people rejoice: but when the wicked beareth rule, the people mourn."*
>
> –Proverbs 29:2

Prayerfully, we—the righteous people of God—will have learned to follow one true Leader, Jesus Christ, rather than just doing our own thing. Only then will His kingdom come and His will be done on earth as it is in heaven!

Takeaway Nugget: What leader are you following?

Foundational Scripture: "*...choose you this day whom ye will serve... but as for me and my house, we will serve the LORD.*" –Joshua 24:15

Week 32

Reclaiming What's Yours!

Read Matthew 4:1-11

Picture two little kids on the playground. One has his very favorite toy that his father bought for him. He's happily playing with it in his hands. Suddenly, the other little kid grabs hold of the toy and snatches it out of the first boy's hands! Can't you just hear what the first kid says?

"Hey, what are you doing? That's not yours! My father bought that for me! It belongs to me! You can't have it; it's mine! Give it back right now!"

Our heavenly Father has bought some things far more precious to us than toys. Through the shed blood of Jesus, He has purchased precious promises that belong to us and, for most of us, the enemy has snatched them right out of our hands. Those promises belong to us, the righteous, and it's time for us to reclaim them by telling the enemy, "Hey, what are you doing? That's not yours! My Father bought that for me! It belongs to me! You can't have it; it's mine! Give it back right now!" It's time to take out the sword of the Spirit, which is the Word of God. For many of us, we need to dust it off, polish it up, and start using it.

We first must know what the precious promises are and begin to declare our right to them through the Word of God. It's time to reclaim them; it's time to take them back. Here are just a few we need to take back:

- Our Health – Using the sword of the Spirit, declaring with authority,

  Beloved, I wish above all things that thou mayest prosper and be in health, even as thy soul prospereth.

  –3 John 1:2

  He sent his word, and healed them, and delivered them from their destructions.

  –Psalm 107:20

- Our Peace – Using the sword of the Spirit, declaring with authority,

  Thou wilt keep him in perfect peace, whose mind is stayed on thee: because he trusteth in thee.

  –Isaiah 26:3

- Our Prosperity – Not just financial, but in all things (prosperous ministry, prosperous home life, prosperous work life, prosperous relationships, etc.). Using the sword of the Spirit, declaring with authority,

  Blessed is the man that walketh not in the counsel of the ungodly, nor standeth in the way of sinners, nor sitteth in the seat of the scornful. But his delight is in the law of the LORD; and in his law doth he meditate day and night. And he shall be like a tree planted by the rivers of water, that bringeth forth his fruit in his season; his leaf also shall not wither; and whatsoever he doeth shall prosper.

  –Psalm 1:1-3

- Our Children – Using the sword of the Spirit, declaring with authority, from Deuteronomy 28:32 and *Prayers that Avail Much* by Germaine Copeland,

  > "Our sons and our daughters shall not be given to another people and our eyes shall not look and fail with longing for them all day long."

We enjoy our children and they shall not go into captivity, in the name of Jesus!

- Our Provision – Using the sword of the Spirit, declaring with authority,

  > *But my God shall supply all your need according to His riches in glory by Christ Jesus.*
  >
  > –Philippians 4:19

- Our Purpose – Using the sword of the Spirit, declaring with authority, God says to me,

  > *"For I know the thoughts that I think toward you, says the LORD, thoughts of peace and not of evil, to give you an expected end."*
  >
  > –Jeremiah 29:11

In Matthew 4:1-11, we have been given the example of how to stand against the enemy and reclaim what is ours. We are to simply do what Jesus did: pick up the sword of the Spirit, which is the Word of God, and wield it by speaking it out loud, believing it and remembering that, by faith, the Word of God accomplishes what it says it will do.

So, when you're on the playground today, remember to take out and use your sword, so that when the bully comes and snatches the gift your Father gave to you, which belongs to you, you can reclaim what's yours!

Takeaway Nugget: As a child of God, I have the authority to reclaim what has already been purchased for me!

Foundational Scripture: *And I will restore to you the years that the locust hath eaten, the cankerworm, and the caterpillar, and the palmerworm, my great army which I sent among you.* –Joel 2:25

Week 33

Brand Name or Generic

We all know what a Dixie® cup is. It's a little, paper cup usually used in the bathroom after brushing your teeth. Or how about a Kleenex®? If you say, "Please hand me a Kleenex®," you will receive a tissue to blow your nose, wipe away a tear or remove makeup. Yet both of these items are known almost universally by their brand names and the names of the companies that make them. There are most certainly other makers of paper cups and tissues, but Dixie® and Kleenex® have become synonymous with their respective products. As the brand name Christian, how are you known?

If someone said, "A Christian is sitting over there," what would they see? Too often, we look more like the generic and act more like the knockoff brand. But what should we look like as the brand name Christian? Just like Kleenex® and Dixie®, we should be known by our Maker, Elohim, as persons of quality, substance and standards. Though we come in different sizes, shapes, styles and colors, there should be some characteristics that identify us by our brand.

All true brand-name Christians should be known by the following:

1. First and foremost, we should exude love. Our love should be evident in our speech and actions. Loving others should be characterized by a selfless desire and effort to put all others first (no

partiality), to be sensitive to their needs and to seek to please them.

Love is longsuffering (patient), kind, does not envy, boast and is not puffed up. Love doesn't behave unseemly, doesn't seek its own, is not easily provoked, thinks no evil; does not rejoice in iniquity, but rejoices in the truth; It bears all things, believes all things, hopes all things, endures all things.

−1 Corinthians 13

2. We should definitely always operate in humility. Humility is defined as a modest or low view of one's own importance; humbleness. It is the complete opposite of pride and selfishness. It is not low self-esteem, but humble people take a step back. They don't have to be noticed or recognized and know how to make a point without demanding or commanding. Humble people listen and observe; they help bring out the best in every conversation or situation.
3. Christians ought to be generous with their time, money, resources and even their love.
4. Christians should be dependable. Our word should mean something. If we tell someone we will do something, we should do it with excellence and accuracy, within a reasonable time, and with a good attitude. We should show up when we say we will be there and notify them if we cannot make it. If we cannot do something, we should simply say, "That is not my area of expertise, but let me see if I can find someone who can."

5. Christians should be consistent. We should not be up and faithful one day, and downtrodden and worried the next. Sure, we have our moments, but remember that we are always being observed to see if we are the real deal, genuine and true. That means that we should exhibit consistency. When people look at us, they should not see double-mindedness, indecisiveness, flip-flopping or, my favorite word, "wishy-washy" behavior. We are to be steady, steadfast, acting in the same way over time, which is the very definition of consistent.
6. Christians should be open, honest, truthful and transparent. We should be full of integrity. People should be able to know that a Christian will tell them the truth in love without wounding or demeaning them. That means that we do not lie, cover or mislead. The honesty and openness of a Christian should exude light and draw others to light and, of course, that light is Jesus!

These are really just a few things that people should see in a Christian. There are so many more characteristics, but mostly we should exude goodness, joy, peace, kindness, faithfulness, love, gentleness, patience, and self-control, which all make up the fruit of the Spirit. This is what the brand name of Christian should be made of and look like. As an end product, we should be durable, reliable, marked by quality, and carry a lifetime warranty! So, as you go about your walk, ask yourself if you are thinking as, speaking as or acting like a brand-name Christian or just a generic knockoff?

Takeaway Nugget: Behave like a Christian.

Foundational Scripture: *Let your light so shine before men, that they may see your good works, and glorify your Father which is in heaven.*
—Matthew 5:16

Week 34

Acts of Love

Read 1 Corinthians 13:4–8a

I remember a day when my pastor, who's also my friend and mentor, came up next to me, put her arm around my waist and gave me a sideways hug. Through that embrace, I felt not only her love, but the pure love of Jesus. She smiled at me, said something humorous and then we each went on our way. When I stop and remember that tiny moment in eternity, I am filled with an overwhelming sense of being loved. How powerful that is! We must never underestimate the power of love. One act of love can change a person in an instant, taking them from a place of sorrow to joy, from disillusionment to hope, or from bondage to freedom.

These are simple acts of love: a smile, a compliment, a word of encouragement, a nod of approval, an offer of help, an unexpected gift, a card, a text or a phone call. These seemingly small gestures can have a powerful, life-changing impact on a person's outlook, perspective, situation or even about how they feel about themselves. We can never know just how profound the effect of a simple act of love can have when coupled with the power and work of the Holy Spirit, who combines His "super" with our "natural" to bring great "supernatural" results. When God is in control, anything we do in Jesus' name, according to His Word and with the blood of Jesus, is magnified and far-reaching.

One definition of love is "the decision to righteously seek the welfare of others." We know from 1 Corinthians 13:4-8a that love, biblically speaking, is not an emotion, but an action. It's something to be carried out and not felt. And while we can feel loved, true love extends out to another—it is "self-forgetting." The Bible teaches it this way.

> *Love suffers long and is kind; love does not envy; love does not parade itself, is not puffed up; does not behave rudely, does not seek its own, is not provoked, thinks no evil; does not rejoice in iniquity, but rejoices in the truth; bears all things, believes all things, hopes all things, endures all things. Love never fails.*
> —1 Corinthians 13:4-8a (NKJV)

Do you hear the action words? Suffers, behaves, seeks, thinks, rejoices, bears, believes, hopes and endures. We are called to put love into action; to shower it upon the lost, the brokenhearted, the lonely, the grieving, the mentally ill, and the hopeless, to name a few. One simple act of love can bring comfort, assurance, affirmation, clarity (where there was confusion) or a stabilizing effect.

I remember a close friend telling me about a time after her divorce, when her son, who was struggling with some depression and anger, was in his room and kind of spaced out. He was visibly disturbed, which was not the norm for him. It was as though a spirit had come over him. Seeing him like that and not really being familiar with spiritual warfare, it scared her. Immediately, the Holy Spirit prompted her to just go over to him, throw her arms around him and hold him in an embrace of a mother's love. She told me that, over the course of a few minutes, he slowly began to calm down and whatever had overtaken him was defeated. Victory, in that moment, came with a simple act of the powerful love of Jesus. I will never forget that.

We know that Satan cannot handle a lover. The love of Jesus is the most powerful force in the universe!

> *"For I am persuaded, that neither death, nor life, nor angels, nor principalities, nor powers, nor things present, nor things to come, nor height, nor depth, nor any other creature, shall be able to separate us from the love of God, which is in Christ Jesus our Lord.*
>
> –Romans 8:38-39

Nothing can stand against the power of love.

Some people call the things I mentioned earlier "random acts of kindness," but we can also call them "acts of love." One definition of kindness in New Testament Greek is "love toward man." While it speaks of God's kindness toward us, we are also called to love our fellow man. We need to slow down and really focus on being exceedingly loving by purposing to practice these acts of love.

On the surface, they might seem like small things, but a kind word spoken to a stranger might shock them out of a plan to commit suicide—not because of what you said, but because of the power of love—the love of Jesus behind your words. Those words imparted the love of Jesus straight into their heart. Jesus is love. People know when you care; people can sense it and sometimes feel it. We all experience this at Christmastime, because that is the time when love was born! The atmosphere is tinged with love. When acts of love are delivered with sincerity, the supernatural power of the Spirit of God does the exceeding abundant above all that you even intended! We might never know the true impact of our small, sincere acts of love on other people, but I believe that God will use them to do the miraculous to uplift others and give them hope! Amen!

Takeaway Nugget: Never underestimate the power of one small act of love.

Foundational Scripture: *And now abide faith, hope, love, these three; but the greatest of these is love.*
–1 Corinthians 13:13 (NKJV)

Week 35

Have You Lost Power?

Because of heavy storms, we often lose power for a day or longer.

I want you to read this:

"Everybody here has power in your home based on your electricity provider. So, you have an electricity provider and that provider gives you power. That power means you can turn on lights, you can plug in appliances. That power makes your life much more livable for you because it's connected to a power source provider. They're not going to come to your house and flip on your light switch, they're not going to come into your house and plug in your appliances. What they have provided is a point of contact. You must flip on your light switch. You must plug in your appliances. You don't plug it in to get power. You plug it in to access power. You already have power, assuming you paid your bills. You already have power; your job is to access that power. And when it comes to your Christian experience with God, you don't have to worry about paying the bill; cause the bill has already been paid. Jesus Christ has already created the link to access God's predetermined programmed will, but that's access through prayer. "(Excerpt from Pastor Tony Evans' Radio Broadcast, 07/24/19)

We suffer from our own personal power outages when we allow life's circumstances to overwhelm us, to stress us out mentally or even to the point where we are sick (physically). In the natural, a power outage occurs when there is a loss of the electrical power network supply to an end user. The connection to the power source is broken. The power supply is still available, but the connection to it has been interrupted.

This is also true in the spiritual. The Holy Spirit is our supply; He is the source of our power. However, when we rely on our own resources, which are powerless, we break the connection which results in an outage. Again, the power supply is still available; we are just no longer tapped into it.

Whenever, in our feeble attempts, we try to take control of our own lives, we are operating in pride and cut off the power supply. If we are not leaning on and crying out to the Holy Spirit for help, we are operating in the dark, just as we are in a power outage. This disconnect is the cause of all of the stress, anxiety and dis-ease we experience. We have no power because we have lost the connection. And truth be told, we're the ones who break the connection.

John 6:63 tells us that it is the spirit that quickens; the flesh profits nothing. The Holy Spirit is the third person of the Trinity. If you are not actively engaged with Him every day, you are in a power outage. The Holy Spirit is the One who empowers you and equips you to overcome the day-to-day pressures and trials to bring us into Christlikeness. He is our Comforter and Advocate who comes alongside to aid us in times of trouble. Without an active, intimate relationship with the Holy Spirit, you have no power to bring glory to or accomplish anything for God.

In John 15:5b NKJV, Jesus said, "for without Me you can do nothing." The only way that we can do anything for God that bears good fruit and allows us to experience His peace is to stay connected to the power source (the vine). And the only way we can do that is through prayer, through reading the Word, through sitting quietly in God's presence, through praise, especially since God inhabits the praises of His people. We also stay connected by humbling ourselves through honest confession of our weaknesses and the understanding that we can't do it (whatever the "it" is) without the Holy Spirit. Every day, we must—at all times—be actively engaged with the third person of the Trinity: the precious Holy Spirit.

So again, I ask you: As you examine your current life and circumstances, have you lost power?

Takeaway Nugget: Stay connected to the power source.

Foundational Scripture: *Abide in me, and I in you. As the branch cannot bear fruit of itself, except it abide in the vine; no more can ye, except ye abide in me. I am the vine, ye are the branches: He that abideth in me, and I in him, the same bringeth forth much fruit: for without me ye can do nothing. If a man abide not in me, he is cast forth as a branch, and is withered; and men gather them, and cast them into the fire, and they are burned. If ye abide in me, and my words abide in you, ye shall ask what ye will, and it shall be done unto you. Herein is my Father glorified, that ye bear much fruit; so shall ye be my disciples.*

–John 15:4-8

Week 36

Giant Rewards

Do you want giant rewards? I know I do. Who wants mediocre or measly rewards in their life? No one! Let me tell you how to get giant rewards.

First, some background from 1 Samuel 17. The Israelite army, headed by King Saul, and the Philistines were faced off in war while camped in the Elah Valley. A champion named Goliath from the Philistine camp taunted and challenged the Israelites to send a man to face off with him in battle. Believing and boasting that no one could defeat him, Goliath taunted them, saying, "Am I not a Philistine and you the servants of Saul? I defy the armies of Israel this day; give me a man, that we may fight." The Israelites were dismayed and greatly afraid when they heard these words. This taunting went on for 40 days.

Meanwhile, David, the youngest of Jesse's eight sons, was commanded by his father to go and take some provisions of food to two of his brothers, who were on the front lines of the battle. David obeyed his father and went to the front lines, met up with his brothers and there he heard this Philistine taunting the Israelite Army. Not being afraid of this bully, he decided to take action against him. That is what we must do.

Satan is a bully who rises up, appearing like a giant, but not really being one. The Word says,

> *Be sober, be vigilant; because your adversary the devil, as a roaring lion, walketh about, seeking whom he may devour.*
>
> –1 Peter 5:8

The men of Israel saw the giant, fled from him and were dreadfully afraid. So, this is what they said.

> *Have ye seen this man that is come up? surely to defy Israel is he come up: and it shall be, that the man who killeth him, the king will enrich him with great riches, and will give him his daughter, and make his father's house free in Israel.*
>
> –1 Samuel 17:25

David was not fazed by this giant at all. And if you are familiar with the story, you know how it ends. David was victorious in killing the giant. If you've never read it, I suggest that you check it out in 1 Samuel 17.

The verse I want to focus on, which spoke to me as I read it, is 1 Samuel 17:25b, which says, and it shall be, that the man who killeth him, the king will enrich with great riches. This spoke to my heart and this is what I got from it. When you kill the giants in your life, the King—the King of Kings will allow you to reap giant rewards! Here's how: We must follow David's example:

David first identified and acknowledged the giant in his life. He said,

For who is this uncircumcised Philistine that he should defy the armies of the living God?
–1 Samuel 17:26b

So, you first have to identify the giants in your life. What giant are you in battle with? What giant is taunting you and boasting that he's going to kill you? Is it fear? An addiction? Your pride? Anger? Unforgiveness? Depression? Lack of trust? You must identify the giant and then acknowledge that you have fed it and helped it grow to the size of a Philistine giant like Goliath. In other words, confess to the Lord what giant(s) you have entertained all your days, that now has a stronghold on you. If you don't know—and many times, we don't know—ask the Holy Spirit to reveal that giant or giants to you.

Next, having first identified the giant, David was ready to confront it. He was annoyed enough by this bully that he declared aloud that this giant was not going to prevail, but would be killed. That word got back to King Saul, who requested a meeting with him. David said,

Let no man's heart fail because of him; thy servant will go and fight with this Philistine.
–1 Samuel 17:32

Saul, looking at David, said,

> *"Thou art not able to go against this Philistine to fight with him: for thou art but a youth, and he a man of war from his youth."*
>
> –1 Samuel 17:33

David ignored that lie from the lips of another. He did not receive the opinion of someone who really knew nothing about him. Stop listening to naysaying friends, relatives and other people who want to tell you, "You'll never get over that addiction" or "You've been fearful all your life, that's never going to change." Shut that noise up!

> *Let the lying lips be put to silence; which speak grievous things proudly and contemptuously against the righteous.*
>
> –Psalm 31:18

You've been declared righteous. Begin to speak aloud what the Word says about you! David put his confidence in the One who would work through him to take the giant out, and you should, too. Declare, "I can do all things through Christ who strengthens me; greater is He who is in me, than he who is in the world."

Seeing that David was serious, Saul clothed David with his armor, a bronze helmet, a coat of mail and a sword. But David was not willing to listen to another about how to take the giant out. Do not let other people tell you how to conquer your giants. Everybody's got an opinion and they think you're entitled to it. Stop listening to people tell you, "Oh, you need to try this <worldly method>" or "You need to come with me to this conference," or "Hey, give me a call and we can talk about your problem." No! Don't be swayed by what others have to say. Be led by the Holy Spirit! Also, stop making excuses for your giants and pampering them. You need to speak,

> *"...let us lay aside every weight, and the sin which doth so easily beset us, and let us run with patience the race that is set before us.*
> –Hebrews 12:1b

David listened to his own heart and determined he didn't need anything but faith. It takes faith to move mountains and giants, not external things like a heavy coat of armor (e.g., worldly methods, intellectual reasoning, or strategies from unanointed books). All you need is faith. All you need to cause a shift in the atmosphere is your voice speaking the Word aloud, coupled with your faith.

We know from the story that David, armed only with faith in the living God, a sling and five smooth stones, took the giant out with the first stone! Now, that may not happen for you the first time, but you keep throwing the other four stones (or as many as it takes) and saying what Jesus said in the wilderness against the devil—"It is written...it is written...it is written." And eventually, the devil will flee (read Luke 4:1-13).

After the giant is conquered and killed, you will reap "giant rewards"! What are they? First, the greatest is that you will have been delivered from a lifelong stronghold! You will also reap elevated faith, peace of mind, and clearer vision because the weight of that giant is gone! That giant has been slain, all because you spoke to it with the Word of God, as David did, saying,

> *Thou comest to me with a sword, and with a spear, and with a shield: but I come to thee in the name of the LORD of hosts, the God of the armies of Israel, whom thou hast defied.*
> –1 Samuel 17:45

David knew that his confidence was in nothing else but the one true living God and that the battle was the Lord's, who will give those giants into your hands! And that's a giant reward!

Takeaway Nugget: Identify the "giant" in your life. Confess it and then cry out to the Lord to help you defeat him.

Foundational Scripture: *Then they cried unto the LORD in their trouble, and he delivered them out of their distresses.*
–Psalm 107:6

Week 37

Thankful for "In"

We are thankful for who God is and for His character—and we should be. We're also thankful for all that God does for us and we should be thankful for that as well. But how thankful are we for what God is doing in us?

We can clearly see who God is; all we have to do is look at a sunrise or just consider the fact that no two snowflakes are the same. We certainly appreciate (or should appreciate) all that God does for us as a provider, protector and so much more. Yet, we get so easily discouraged when we don't see change in us. We say things like, "Why is it taking so long to be delivered from anger?" "God, when will I walk in total forgiveness?" "When will the stronghold of addiction be broken off of me?", and "How long before I experience my physical healing?" Nobody can whine, moan, groan or complain like a child of God! We just need to be more thankful for what God is doing in us and be patient.

Patience is defined as "the capacity to accept or tolerate delay, trouble or suffering without getting angry or upset." And we've been reminded that all that whining, moaning, groaning and complaining does not move God. Only our faith moves Him. Only our faith talk moves Him, as well as the angels who, on our behalf, heed the Word when we speak it.

> *Bless the LORD, ye his angels, that excel in strength, that do his commandments, hearkening unto the voice of his word.*
> —Psalm 103:20

Let me ask a couple of questions. Men, are you still playing with little toy cars today? Ladies, are you still playing with Barbie® dolls? No! Of course not! The point is, we are not at the same level of maturity we were when we were children. Just as we are no longer at the same level as we were when we were children, prayerfully by this time, we are also no longer at the same level or place spiritually. We must believe that God is still doing work in us and wait patiently.

James 1:4 says,

> *But let patience have her perfect work, that ye may be perfect and entire, wanting nothing.*

In this text, the word perfect means "mature." God is growing us up, and He is doing the work. In this passage, perfect in the Greek means, "cheerful (or hopeful) endurance; constancy, continuance; waiting." We are to wait cheerfully and hopefully as God does His work. Whatever struggles, whatever issues we have, they didn't grow overnight (your soul has been working overtime); so those issues will not go away just like that. We must let the Holy Spirit work in us and finish what He has started.

The Word says,

> *Being confident of this very thing, that he which hath begun a good work in you will perform it until the day of Jesus Christ:*
> –Philippians 1:6

For that, we really need to be thankful. Perform, in the Greek, means "fulfill further (completely), execute, accomplish, do, finish, make perfect." And remember, perfect means mature. God is not finished yet; He wants to develop character in us and we have to allow that work to take place. He's telling us, "Don't give up, but wait on the Lord." God has your situation under control, beloved.

> *The LORD is good unto them that wait for him, to the soul that seeketh him. It is good that a man should both hope and quietly wait for the salvation of the LORD.*
> –Lamentations 3:25-26

And while you wait, be still, be in the Word, be serving, be prayerful, be faithful, sing, obey, worship, pay your tithes, study, rejoice, abide in His presence and stay encouraged. I, for one, am thankful for what God is doing in me. I may not like the waiting and sometimes I get discouraged, but I know that God is not a man that He should lie. So, like the old-timey song says, "God said it. I believe it. I'm gonna take Him at His word." I hope you will do the same. Remember to praise Him until you dance out of your clothes and always remember to be thankful. Amen!

Takeaway Nugget: When you see a character change that God has made in you, a special kind of worship takes place because you know that only He could have done it!

Foundational Scripture: *O magnify the LORD with me, and let us exalt his name together. I sought the LORD, and he heard me, and delivered me from all my fears.*
–Psalm 34:3-4

Week 38

Dried Up and Dirty

I was given the gift of a poinsettia one Christmas. After several months, it started looking pretty pitiful with dead branches, almost no leaves and was dry as a bone. I probably should have thrown it away; I received suggestions to that effect, that it was time to do just that. However, I am so glad that I didn't. I could see just a little bit of green peeking out from just a couple of the branches. There was a glimmer of hope for this neglected, abused little plant. Sadly, I, as its gardener, neglected it for a long time and was close to throwing it out.

Some of you may feel like that plant—dried up and hopeless, wondering if God is ready to throw you away. But praise God, that as His child, He sees and knows your potential, and the plans He has for you. He wants you to prosper and is not out to harm you, but to bring you to an expected end. He knows that there is fruit in you. He sees that little bit of green peeking out. He sees exactly what you need and doesn't want to throw you away.

After I decided to water the plant, lo and behold, it started to come back to life! That's exactly how we are. Sometimes, we just need to be watered. Jesus said in John 15:1-2,

> *"I am the true vine, and my Father is the husbandman. Every branch in me that beareth not fruit he taketh away: and every branch that beareth fruit, he purgeth it, that it may bring forth more fruit.*

Our Gardener wants to hold on to us and for us to hold on to Him so that we will bear more fruit.

> *"If ye abide in me, and my words abide in you, ye shall ask what ye will, and it shall be done unto you."*
> –John 15:7

He sees the potential in us and invites us to come and get watered. Jesus is the Word and the Word, as living water, cleanses and refreshes us. He told his disciples, "You are already clean because of the word which I have spoken to you." You see, they had already been abiding with Him in a close, intimate relationship. And so are we if we're in the Word and in prayer every day. Since the Word is likened to water—the living water, it washes us and cleanses us all the more as we spend time in it.

Let's look at it this way. If the Word washes and cleanses you every time you read it, if you stay away from it (by not reading it), you'll get dirty again. Let's say that the bathtub is the Word. The more you get in the bathtub, the cleaner you'll be. That's why, of course, you take a bath or shower every day, so you can get clean again. The water is the Word; the more you immerse yourself in it, the cleaner you'll get. For every day that you don't bathe—every day that you don't read the Word, the dirt of life accumulates more and more, and you'll need to be washed again.

Chuck Swindoll wrote, "Just as clean, fresh water cleanses our bodies, God's written word washes us clean deep down inside our souls. It purifies our thoughts, scrubs our motives and cleans our conscience as we absorb it and obey its truths." In Ephesians 5:26, this is known as the "washing of the water by the word."

Go a few days without any Word or prayer. You may think you're doing okay, but let a co-worker say something the wrong way or someone cut you off on the road. Or, all of a sudden, you start feeling down and don't know why. Where did that come from?! It's because you've disconnected from the lifeline, the water source. In the natural, you can go a good while without food, but you can only live for three days without water. It's the same with the Word. After three days, you will be very close to perishing spiritually.

We are told to pray without ceasing, to meditate on the Word day and night, to keep it before our eyes and in our heart. Make it a practice to spend time with Jesus in prayer, reading His word and fellowshipping with Him every day to stay watered. Jesus is the Way, the Truth and the Life. The truth will make you free, but it's the Word that gives you life! Water yourself with that life every single day so that you don't become dried up and dirty!

Takeaway Nugget: Sometimes, we feel dried up and dirty, but if Jesus is your Savior and Lord, and you are a true child of God, the heavenly Father will never throw you away.

Foundational Scripture: *"You are already clean because of the word which I have spoken to you. Abide in Me, and I in you. As the branch cannot bear fruit of itself, unless it abides in the vine, neither can you, unless you abide in Me."*
–John 15:3-4 (NKJV)

Week 39

Call on the Lord

The LORD is near to all who call upon Him, To all who call upon Him in truth.
–Psalm 145:18 NKJV

I heard a radio ad for a mental health hotline that said, "If you need help, call this number." There's a hotline for everything today! But, I'm here to tell you that in the kingdom of God, there's a hotline number for whatever you're dealing with.

If you're struggling with Danger, dial 1-800-Psalm 91

If you're struggling with Anxiety, dial 1-800-Philippians 4:6-7

If you're struggling with Fear, dial 1-800-Isaiah 41:10

If you're struggling with Worry, dial 1-800-Psalm 23

If you're struggling with Acceptance, dial 1-800-Ephesians 1:6

No matter what it is, there is an 800 number for it. Call the helpline:

There's:

- Help for hurting
- Hope for the helpless
- Grace for the groaning
- Joy for the jilted
- Comfort for the confused
- Temperance (look it up) for the tempted
- A friend for the friendless
- Love for the lonely
- Strength for the strung out
- Faith for the fearful
- Wisdom for the foolish
- And much, much more—just call Him up

It's a direct line. Open 24 hours, 7 days a week, 365 days a year.

There's no busy signal.

There's no "Please hold."

There's no voicemail—you'll get a live connection to the living God.

There's no "You're caller #15 in the queue." With Jesus, you're #1 every time. He's always available when you call; you'll get right through. The line is open.

So call in, call out, call up, call early, call late—just call!

> *And call upon me in the day of trouble: I will deliver thee, and thou shalt glorify me.*
> –Psalm 50:15

He shall call upon me, and I will answer him…
–Psalm 91:15a

In the day of my trouble I will call upon thee: for thou wilt answer me.
–Psalm 86:7

Takeaway Nugget: Call upon the Lord, even in the middle of the night. He is always awake. He neither slumbers nor sleeps.

Foundational Scripture: *And it shall come to pass that whoever calls on the name of the LORD shall be saved.*
–Joel 2:32a (NKJV)

Week 40

Christmas AfterMATH

How did your last Christmas add up? Did you get the number of gifts you wanted or expected? Was the number of family or friends you hoped for around your dinner table? There is only one number that really adds up—well, actually make that three in one—and that is Father, Son and Holy Spirit! No matter how you calculate it, life without Jesus is a big fat zero!

Every December, Christians celebrate the greatest gift to mankind, the birth of our Savior and Lord, Jesus Christ, who has already given us everything we could ever want or need. Here are just a few of the infinite blessings His birth, life, death and resurrection provide:

- Forgives all your iniquities, transgressions and sins (past, present and future)
- Heals all your diseases
- Redeems your life from destruction
- Crowns you with lovingkindness
- Satisfies your mouth with good things (His Word)
- Executes righteousness and justice when you are oppressed
- Delivers you from the snare of the fowler
- Covers you with His feathers
- Gives His angels charge over you
- Will be with you in trouble
- Satisfies you with long life
- Orders your steps

- Gives grace to the humble
- Provides brand new mercies each morning
- Hems you in behind and before
- Supplies all your needs and fills your barn
- Strengthens you on your bed of illness
- Will not forget you
- Inscribed you on the palm of His hands
- Keeps your walls continually before Him (Isaiah 49:16)
- Whose kindness shall not depart from you
- Whose covenant of peace shall not be removed
- Lifts up a standard against your enemies who come in like a flood
- Proclaims liberty to your captivity
- Opens the prison of your bondage
- Heals your broken heart
- Gives you beauty for ashes
- Gives power when you're weak
- Increases strength when you have no might
- Guards all your bones
- Restores your soul
- Leads you beside still waters
- Comforts you with His rod and staff
- Anoints your head with oil
- Will not let the sun strike you by day nor the moon by night
- Produces the fruit of the Spirit of God in you
- Opens your eyes to see and ears to hear
- Convicts you of sin
- Rewards your obedience
- Shines light on your heart and illuminates the Word of God

- Gives you rest when you're weary and burdened
- Numbers the hairs on your head
- Is the God who sees you
- Leads you in the way everlasting
- Preserves you from violent men
- Deals bountifully with you
- Brings your prodigal sons and daughters from afar
- Loves you with an everlasting love
- Knows the plans He has for you
- Promises never to leave you nor forsake you
- Lifts up His countenance upon you and gives you peace!

Takeaway Nugget: If you have Jesus, you have everything, and that adds up to one full abundant life! Let's continue to worship the Lord of Lords, King of Kings, the Great I AM and our Savior, Jesus, not just at Christmastime, but always!

Foundational Scripture: *Thanks be to God for His indescribable gift!*
–2 Corinthians 9:15 (NKJV)

Week 41

Gifts From My Father

I ran across some gifts that my father bought me and it made me smile. There was a pair of decorative glass dolphins, a mug with a joke about diet soda, and a set of stoneware dishes. Seeing these items brought back warm memories and got me reflecting. And while these are nice little gifts and I cherish them, the most important gifts that my father ever gave me were his love, his attention, his time and his presence.

Fathers, the Lord is speaking to you to encourage you and support you in your relationship with your children, especially your daughters. Your daughters need to hear from you. They need to know that you love them. When was the last time you actually put your arm around your daughter or pulled her close to your side and simply said, "I love you"? I am puzzled that so many people have such a hard time actually saying, "I love you," yet those three simple words can have a profound impact on a person's life, especially a young person and even more, especially a young girl.

I have read of and heard so many accounts where people have said, "My father never told me he loved me." I find it interesting that some say, "Oh, I know my father loved me; he just never said it." My thought is, how do you know he loved you? The worldly saying is, "Actions speak louder than words." In some instances, maybe they do, but as believers, we know that words have great power. God spoke the world into existence with His words. He also sent His Word to heal and save us. Words have lasting impact. People who've been abused will tell you that their physical wounds healed, but the hurtful, damaging words that were spoken still ring in their ears and have left a lasting mark. Words have great power. Fathers, tell your daughters and your sons, "I love you." Say it.

Daughters need to hear that they are beautiful, not that they look beautiful. Anyone can be made to look beautiful. Tell them that they are beautiful. Acknowledge and tell them that they are smart, that you see their talents and gifts, and that you know that they can excel in whatever it is that God has planned for them.

I once read about a 27-year-old female dietician from New York, who hanged herself in her apartment. She left two suicide notes, and in one of them she said, "I often felt detached while in a room full of my favorite people." People need to know that they are loved. Without question, they need to know the love of God, which surpasses any love we will ever know. They also need to know that their parents love them. How will they know unless you tell them?

A father can have a profound impact on a girl's life, both negatively and positively. Girls get validation from their father. Just knowing that you are loved can make all the difference in a girl's life. Here is the challenge to every father reading this today: Tell your daughters you love them. Call them up today and say, "You may not have heard this much or at all from me, but I love you." Take that one step of obedience and watch God, who is love, open up that relationship and breathe new life into it. Do it; it just might save your daughter's life. And yours.

Takeaway Nugget: Tell someone you love them.

Foundational Scripture: *And now abide faith, hope, love, these three; but the greatest of these is love.*
–1 Corinthians 13:13 (NKJV)

Week 42

Help Me, Lord!

Help - to give or provide what is necessary to accomplish a task or satisfy a need; render assistance or aid

We all need help at one time or another. Unfortunately, we too often turn to the wrong source for that help. Most times, we are asking other human beings, some of whom, in all fairness, operate in wisdom, but generally cannot offer the best solution because they are not God. The only time they can is if they have sought the Holy Spirit and are being led by Him. Our best source of help comes from the Lord.

The Word says,

> *"Call unto me, and I will answer thee, and show thee great and mighty things, which thou knowest not."*
> –Jeremiah 33:3

Also, he tells us plainly,

> *I will strengthen you, Yes, I will help you, I will uphold you with My righteous right hand."*
> –Isaiah 41:10b (NKJV)

The Holy Spirit is our helper; that's His name. So, help is available to us at any time. The question is, are we actually calling out to the Lord for help? And when we do, what does it sound like?

What do you say when you ask the Lord for help?

1. Do you say, "Lord, I need you to help me find a way to generate income or find a second job so I can save more money, pay some bills or just have a little extra to do some things I enjoy" or do you say, "Lord, if it is Your will that I have a different job, order my steps toward new employment"? Or perhaps, you say, "Lord, help me learn to be content in every situation, whether well fed or hungry, whether living in plenty or in want. Help me, Lord, in everything to give thanks, for this is Your will in Christ Jesus concerning me." (Philippians 4:12, 1 Thessalonians 5:18)
2. Do you say, "Lord, I am working as hard as I can on this job, but these people are getting on my nerves and my supervisor is riding me and I feel as though I can't do anything right; there's always some criticism. You've got to get me out of here," or do you say, "Lord, help me to see myself truly the way you see me in this situation. Help me to see if there is something I am doing or not doing in my work that needs to change"?
3. Do you say, "Lord, my relative or my friend has hurt and offended me. Help me figure out what to say so that I can set them straight and let them know that they can't just treat me like that. I'm angry and wounded, and I need You to help me make them understand," or do you say, "Lord help me to forgive them, for they knew not what they

were doing? Help me to choose the narrow way, humble myself and turn the other cheek. Help me to choose to forgive them 70 X 7 as you heal my emotions so that they will match the words of forgiveness I chose to verbalize." (See Luke 23:34, Matthew 18:22)

4. Do you say, "Lord, help me show my husband the error of his ways. He's not the priest of our home that he needs to be and I need you to help me to tell him that" or do you say, "Help me to trust in the Lord with all mine heart and lean not to mine own understanding, but in all my ways acknowledge You and You shall direct my paths"? In so doing, do you then say, "Help me Lord to take this matter to my prayer closet and help me find the right Scriptures that will target the situation to give me wisdom, understanding, and peace while I wait for You to bring conviction to my husband that results in change, all without my having to speak a word"? (See Proverbs 3:5-6)
5. Do you say, "Lord, help me with my children. They're sullen, angry, disrespectful and uncooperative. I don't understand their behavior. Help me find somewhere I can send them—a church, a school, an athletic program or extra-curricular activity I can involve them in so that they will become more responsible" or do you say, "Help me, Lord, to confess and repent for my lack of parenting; help me to understand my children, to listen to them and not provoke them to wrath, but bring them up in the training and admonition of the Lord. Help me to want to spend quality time with them and then make that time every day to

connect with them. This is my earnest prayer?" (See Ephesians 6:4)

When we cry out for help, often we are not asking for the right help. The Bible says in James 4:2b-3 NKJV,

> *You do not have because you do not ask. You ask and do not receive, because you ask amiss, that you may spend it on your pleasures.*

We must always ask for help according to the will of God and that is our problem. We are not asking in line with God's plan, His will, His agenda. We are often asking for things that will appease our flesh. God is not going to grant our pleas if they are carnal or soulish. For example, you cannot pray for God to give you a house that someone is already living in if it's not up for sale. You can pray foolishly for God to cause them to need to move, but unless that is God's plan and will for their lives, you're not getting that house!

God left us His Holy Spirit, the third person of the trinity, to help us, to guide us and lead us in a plain path that leads to righteousness and peace. He expects us to use wisdom when we cry out. Granted, there are times when we don't know what to cry out. That's when you can simply say, "Holy Spirit, help me to be still and know what you would even have me ask for right now." If you would be still and listen, the Holy Spirit will help you formulate the perfect prayer, which will then be answered, in God's timing. It will bring exactly what you need. So, be encouraged, beloved; help is on the way when you ask according to the Way!

Takeaway Nugget: Pray the "right"eous way.

Foundational Scripture: *In all thy ways acknowledge him, and he shall direct thy paths.*
–Proverbs 3:6

Week 43

Imitators of God

We are to imitate Christ and model our lives after Him. This word, translated as "imitators" or "followers," is mimetes (mim-ay-tes) in Greek, the root of the English word mimic. It has the positive meaning: emulating a pattern set by an admired mentor. It is used seven times in the New Testament to advocate following or emulating certain early church leaders, Christ, and, ultimately, God.

A child imitating his or her parent is the most natural thing in the world. It's how children learn everything—from brushing their teeth to putting away toys to treating others with respect. Young children want to grow up to be like their parents, and they will often pretend to be their parents—trying on their parents' shoes, wearing their hats, etc. It's an important part of childhood play as they imitate what they see in their parents. This is the type of mimicry that Paul alludes to in Ephesians 5.

If you were accused of being a Christian, would there be enough evidence to convict you? Are you imitating your heavenly Father or another father—the devil, the father of lies? Sin is sin to God; there are no degrees. It all grieves His heart, but we have difficulty accepting that. We want to categorize sin. So, let's go back to the question: If you were accused of being a Christian, would there be enough evidence to convict you? Ponder these questions:

If a cashier gave you sixteen cents too much in change, would you go back to return it?

Do you reason that it's okay to take a few paper clips or pencils from the work supply cabinet?

If you come up on a small group of your brothers and sisters in Christ who are speaking negatively about another member, do you join in or speak up to them with a gentle rebuke?

How are you when driving? If you're running late and someone has their turn signal on to merge into your lane, do you speed up and not let them in? Do you exceed the speed limit, reasoning that it's okay because "I'm running late"?

If two of you agree to meet at 5:30, do you show up at 6:00 without contacting the other party, arrogantly thinking, "Well, they'll just have to wait"?

It's easy to reason out these seemingly small things. Some people, even other Christians, will make fun of you for doing these "right" things, thinking of you as "self-righteous" or a "goody two-shoes," but God sees these things differently. He expects obedience in all things ("if you love Me, you will obey Me"). These kinds of things speak to your character and ultimately your reverence for God, who sets the standards. And what's really important is that these are the kinds of things that witness to unbelievers because they are watching.

They're not expecting you to commit murder or steal, but the evidence that you are a Christian is in these small, everyday things. Oftentimes, that's what stands out to them the most. I once called over a waitress who had forgotten to include my beverage on the bill. She was very young and she looked at me quizzically before asking, "Why would you point that out to me since I forgot it?" And I replied, "Because it's the right thing to do." I was as puzzled by her remarks to me as she was by mine to her.

As Christians, we are to be set apart in all we say and do. So, the next time you're tempted not to return the grocery cart to the stall, give it a thought. No, God is not expecting perfection, but He is expecting you to be an imitator of Him as His beloved child.

Takeaway Nugget: Whose watching you?

Foundational Scripture: *Therefore be imitators of God as dear children.*
–Ephesians 5:1 (NKJV)

Week 44

Missing Puzzle Piece

You probably don't often think of this, but if you were gone—not necessarily by dying, but maybe you moved out of town and are no longer physically present in your church community, or you left a job. If you were no longer where you used to be or where you are supposed to be, in other words, "out of pocket," someone would miss you. You would be the missing piece to someone's puzzle. That is how important you are.

God created each one of us. We are uniquely designed and specially crafted with personality, characteristics, facial features, body shape, gifts, skills, abilities, talents, dreams, visions and temperament. This is what the psalmist says about that:

> *For You formed my inward parts; You covered me in my mother's womb. I will praise You, for I am fearfully and wonderfully made; Marvelous are Your works, and that my soul knows very well. My frame was not hidden from You, When I was made in secret, and skillfully wrought in the lowest parts of the earth.*
>
> –Psalm 139:13-15 NKJV

You were skillfully wrought, "worked into shape by artistry or effort." You were handcrafted by almighty God! So, don't ever think that you don't matter. You are a masterpiece in God's eyes.

When you are missing, it matters. It matters to God and it matters to the people in your life. You matter to someone, but most of all, even if you think that no one would miss you, you matter to God. You even matter to people who you have not met yet. There are people who are waiting to meet you whose path you were created to cross. This is why God wants you saved and made free so that you can complete the life puzzle that He created. When you're out of purpose, the puzzle isn't complete. That's how much your life matters. No part of the puzzle is insignificant and just as in the picture here, when your piece is missing, it leaves a gap—a lack.

No whole is great even if one of its parts is missing. Only altogether do we make one perfect picture and no part is insignificant or even greater than the whole.

Read this passage of Scripture:

> *But now are they many members, yet but one body. And the eye cannot say unto the hand, I have no need of thee: nor again the head to the feet, I have no need of you. Nay, much more those members of the body, which seem to be more feeble, are necessary: And those members of the body, which we think to be less honorable, upon these we bestow more abundant honor; and our uncomely parts have more abundant comeliness. For our comely parts have no need: but God hath tempered the body together, having given more abundant honor to that part which lacked. That there should be no schism in the body; but that the members should have the same care one for another. And whether one*

member suffer, all the members suffer with it; or one member be honored, all the members rejoice with it.
–1 Corinthians 12:20-26

So, just remember that you are an important part of the body. As one puzzle piece, you matter to the whole puzzle, and without you, the puzzle is not complete—your piece—your life matters. You have purpose and God has a plan for your life. So, show up where you're supposed to be—yielded, willing, humble and submitted, saying to the Father, "Here am I, the puzzle piece that you uniquely crafted, ready to be used for Your glory!"

Takeaway Nugget: Every life was created for a unique purpose.

Foundational Scripture: *"Before I formed you in the womb I knew you; Before you were born I sanctified you; I ordained you a prophet to the nations."*
–Jeremiah 1:5 (NKJV)

Week 45

Six Million Dollar Man

> "Steve Austin - Astronaut. A man barely alive. Gentlemen, we can rebuild him. We have the technology; we have the capability to make the world's first bionic man. Steve Austin will be that man. Better than he was before—better, better, stronger, faster."
>
> *The Six Million Dollar Man*, 1974-1978 *

You - Priceless Child of God.

A person barely alive. (Remember, before Christ, you are a walking dead person). Your heart, your spirit, was changed immediately upon salvation, but your soul is still bound and even now some may feel barely alive.

Ladies and Gentlemen, El Elyon can rebuild you. He has the technology. He has the capability to make you a new person, a new creation in Christ.

You will be that person.

Better than you were before—better, stronger, healthier, smarter, wiser.

God can make you over anew. God gently nudges you to choose life.

I call heaven and earth to record this day against you, that I have set before you life and death, blessing and cursing: therefore choose life, that both thou and thy seed may live.

–Deuteronomy 30:19

God is a gentleman; He will never force you to accept His offer of salvation, which is why He gave us a free will. He does, however, invite you to choose Him; therefore, choose life!

You can give God all your broken pieces and let Him rebuild you. Give Him all your pain, all your fears, all your plans, all your doubts, all your disappointments, all your striving. How? I'm glad you asked. By humbly crying out that you are a sinner in need of a Savior. Listen to what He is trying to say to you about you. Your honest acceptance of the soul-sick person you've become is what He needs you to admit so that He can strip you of all that junk causing your inner torment and misery, manifesting outwardly. Once you humbly cry out, He can then rebuild you, so that you will be better than you were before—better, stronger, healthier, smarter, wiser. You'll not just be a six-million-dollar man, you'll be a priceless, invaluable, glorious masterpiece ready to be used for His service to draw others to Him!

Takeaway Nugget: If you need to be "rebuilt," God is willing and able to do it!

Foundational Scripture: *Therefore if any man be in Christ, he is a new creature: old things are passed away; behold, all things are become new.*

—2 Corinthians 5:17

* For you younger folks, Google or go to YouTube and search for the intro to *The Six Million Dollar Man* (It's about 1.5 minutes long)

Week 46

What Shall I Render?

What shall I render unto the LORD for all his benefits toward me?
–Psalm 116:12

One of the definitions of render is, "to give in return or retribution; give back, restore; reflect, echo; to give in acknowledgment of dependence or obligation; to pay; to do (a service) for another.

What can we do or give back to the Lord for all He has done for us? What can we give back to God? God is sovereign and all-sufficient, the completely self-existing One who needs nothing. Because of who He is, His love for us is unconditional. Yet, what can we do to show our love for Him?

I beseech you therefore, brethren, by the mercies of God, that ye present your bodies a living sacrifice, holy, acceptable unto God, which is your reasonable service.
–Romans 12:1

That's just reasonable, expected, nothing above the norm. Though we could never pay our Lord back for all that He is to us and all that He has done, nor does He expect us to, He does tell us in His Word that, "If you love me, keep my commandments." How can we render to the Lord? Here are just a few simple things that it might look like:

1. Offering up to Him our worship and our praise even when we don't feel like it. It's called a sacrifice of praise.
2. We can allow Him to stretch us far beyond our comfort zone and to trust Him even when it makes us feel nervous inside. We can remove, as my pastor once said to me, the self-limitations. We can resist falling immediately into the "Moses-syndrome," when he tried to convince God that he wasn't the right man for the job. We must instead trust that God will work through us.
3. We can forgive when it doesn't seem reasonable and certainly doesn't feel good or right.
4. We can sit with and just listen to those really, really long-winded friends without being antsy, fidgety or making gestures that suggest you want to get up and go.
5. Make a generous donation when you know you just can't spare the money. Begin to tithe, even though at the beginning, it doesn't make sense as you look at your budget and finances.
6. When the Lord asks you to, you can give away that precious purchase or that thing that you just bought for yourself. When He asks you to part with it, you can give it away without complaining.
7. We can resist the urge to judge others, to analyze them and their behavior and just be supportive, loving, understanding, kind and pray for what

discernment is telling us their need is. This is possible if we just remove the plank from our own eye.

8. Think of others often. A long time ago, I read something by Joyce Meyer who suggested that every time you find yourself thinking about yourself, be aware of it and then stop and pray for someone else.

What do all of these things have in common? They are simple acts characterized by a laid-down life, a flesh-crucified life, devoid of what I want, what I need, how I feel. A life that lives for God and others, putting Him and others first. It is an ongoing process of sanctification.

What does it take to do this? It takes crying out to the Lord to reveal the strongholds in our lives, then acknowledging them and owning them without that "the devil made me do it" mentality. It takes being truthful with yourself in the inward parts, the truthfulness that leads to godly sorrow and repentance. It also requires reading, studying, speaking and meditating on the Word, along with having the desire to be free. It's an act of our will to make changes with the help of the Holy Spirit by yielding, surrendering to and obeying the leading and prompting of the Holy Spirit. We have to want to be different. We must pray to God to help us. That is why He sent the third person of the Trinity. God knew that we would not be able to change ourselves and that we would need help to do it. What a kind, loving God that is!

Takeaway Nugget: Today, in your quiet time, ask yourself this: What shall I render to the Lord for all His benefits toward me? What, what shall I render; what shall I give?

Foundational Scripture: *I beseech you therefore, brethren, by the mercies of God, that ye present your bodies a living sacrifice, holy, acceptable unto God, which is your reasonable service.*
–Romans 12:1

Week 47

What Will They Remember?

I once watched a very short video clip of a baby getting her hair shampooed, probably for her very first time. The child was beautiful; she had these big black eyes and the sweetest, most pleasant expression on her face. That video mesmerized me and struck a chord in me that I almost couldn't explain. It made me think of how great a responsibility parents, and those of us in the village, have to nurture and protect these precious little ones over who we have been made to be stewards.

The word success is defined as "the accomplishment of an aim or purpose; the attainment of wealth, favor, or eminence." The world defines success in terms of achieving, usually something tangible: a prominent position or title in employment (manager, director, CEO); a raise or high salary; the top seller for a given year; the most touchdowns ever made in a season. These are all things that can be measured in finite terms.

But God sees success very differently and we should see it as such when we think of the impact we have on our children. What will they remember? When they look back on you as a parent, what will they remember? What, in their eyes, will have made you a successful parent? Will they define your success in relation to your work or career? Most of the time, children have little or no idea of what their parents even do. Will they have found you successful because you were a great cook or because you played a mean game of gin rummy? Possibly, if those things were true of you, but the thing that will have had the most impact on them is the time that you spent with them and the positive attention you paid to them with your encouragement, affirming words and genuine interest in what interested them. Some of my fondest memories are of my parents and me sitting at the dining room table, playing board games. Prayerfully, they will remember you as the parent who modeled Jesus' example of how we are to live.

These are the things they will mention when they say, "I have the best mom" or "my dad is the greatest!" They will be talking about how you cared about them or took time to teach them simple things. They'll be talking about the hugs you gave them for no reason or the stories you read to them. They'll be talking about how you pointed them to solutions to their problems from the Word of God. Those are the things they'll remember, but only if you do them! The nurturing of your children has to be intentional and consistent. Think hard about the impact that your life is having on your children. Then ask yourself honestly, "What will they remember?"

Takeaway Nugget: What will my children remember about my being a "successful" parent?

Foundational Scripture: *Lo, children are an heritage of the LORD: and the fruit of the womb is his reward.*
–Psalm 127:3

Week 48

What's Christmas to You?

So many people have such interesting ideas of what Christmas is to them. I once talked with a woman who said, "Yes, we celebrate Christmas. We pick up a tree and exchange gifts; so aside from the spiritual aspect, we do celebrate it." I enjoyed hearing about her culture, but I thought to myself, "There is no other aspect to Christmas except the spiritual one." For many non-spiritual people who celebrate Christmas, as the song implies, to them it's about Santa, putting up a tree, The Grinch, decorating the house with Christmas lights, Frosty the Snowman, chopping down a tree, eggnog, material gifts and presents, Rudolph the Red-Nosed Reindeer and baking Christmas cookies.

And while there is nothing wrong with those things, in and of themselves, that's not what Christmas is about and that's not what Christmas is to me.

So, let me tell you what Christmas means to me:

- It's the celebration of the birth of my Savior, of one who came to rescue me and us out of darkness. He made Himself known to me personally so that I could be reconciled back to my heavenly Father and become a child of God; no longer an object of wrath.
- It's a time of gratitude for lifting up and thanking Jesus for snatching me from the hand of the enemy in various forms: depression, ignorance of the Word, physical symptoms and ailments, confusion, mental

and emotional torment, bondage to negative thinking, pride and self-reliance, unproductive habits and so much more, and to remember that because of Jesus, I don't have to live the way I used to!

- It's a time for me to acknowledge that yes, God has a plan and purpose for all of our lives and that He will prepare us for the work and help us to grow up into it as we yield to the reshaping of our character.
- Christmas is a time to give in service to others in many ways—to listen to someone who is hurting, to visit a lonely friend, to pray and intercede for the lost, to share a meal with an estranged family member, to financially bless someone in need, to open my home in hospitality or to sacrifice my time and plans for someone else.
- It's a time to reflect upon the great I AM being there in whatever situation I find myself. I'm never alone and that I can run into the comforting, all-encompassing arms whenever I feel lonely, attacked, misunderstood or sad. With Jesus and with His help, I am an overcomer.
- It's a time for me to thank the Holy Spirit, my Helper, who will guide me in wisdom in all situations as I lean on and ask for His help.
- It's a time for connecting with family and friends, sharing memories and just enjoying each other's company without texting or technology, but being present in that moment and truly just enjoying the fellowship with each other.

And there were in the same country shepherds abiding in the field, keeping watch over their flock by night… And the angel said unto them, Fear not: for, behold, I bring you good tidings of great joy, which shall be to all people."
–Luke 2:8, 10

I read from a devotional in reference to the verse above about how God could have first announced the birth of His son to Caesar Augustus, the reigning Roman emperor or to King Herod, the king at the time of Jesus' birth, or even to the religious leaders of the day, but that is not what happened. God first announced the birth of Jesus to shepherds. The devotional reading went on to say that we tend to romanticize the shepherds along with everyone else in the Christmas story, but we don't understand who they were.

In that culture, shepherds lived at the bottom of the social ladder.

Shepherds were so despised that their testimonies were not even allowed in a court of law. Shepherds did the work that no one else wanted to do. They worked hard, but they were perceived as unclean because they could not observe the ceremonial hand washings. They were the outcasts, the nobodies.

The only people less regarded than shepherds were those suffering from leprosy. Yet God chose to announce His news to some shepherds in the fields as they kept watch over their flocks at night. This was the modus operandi of Jesus, from birth to death. He always appealed to the outcast, to the common, to the ordinary. And that should give hope to ordinary people like us.

I like how a writer summed up Christmas in a devotional:

> "Christ came to this earth. God came near to you so you can come near to Him—to give your life purpose and meaning, to forgive you of your sins, and to give you the hope of Heaven beyond the grave. Christmas is not about tinsel or shopping or presents. Christmas is not about the gifts under the tree. Rather, Christmas is about the gift that was given on the tree when Christ died there for our sins and gave us the gift of eternal life."

So beloved, as you go about your Christmas busyness, try to focus on what Christmas really means to you, And for me, it's a time to remember that love was born into our world that day to change it forever and secure a place in Him, both now and forevermore to all those who call the name of Jesus—Wonderful, Counsellor, The mighty God, The everlasting Father and The Prince of Peace!

Takeaway Nugget: When celebrating your next Christmas, create special memories centered on the true meaning of Christmas: Jesus!

Foundational Scripture: *For unto you is born this day in the city of David a Savior, which is Christ the Lord.*
–Luke 2:11

Week 49

Who's Got You Covered?

I had a most unusual experience early one morning as I stopped at a well-known grocery store. Though it was early, it was daylight. As I was putting my groceries into my trunk, I stood between my cart and the trunk. Suddenly, without my noticing at first, a man holding a cup of coffee approached me. This is the conversation that took place:

Him: I'll take that cart.
Me: Why? There are plenty of carts in the store!
Him: That's okay; I'll wait.
Me: I'd rather you didn't.
Him: Why's that?
Me: Because I'm feeling rushed.
Him: I'm not rushing you.

After waiting for me to finish loading my groceries, he took my empty cart. When I got in the car, I thought hard about what had just happened. While I wasn't unnerved by the incident, I was pondering the reason for it. I asked God and continued to listen. Fortunately, there was a mature saint and friend at work who had wisdom and great discernment in both spiritual and natural things. I shared the incident with her, and she offered me interesting perspectives on what had taken place.

She began to view it from a safety standpoint. He had a potential weapon (the cup of coffee). He was testing the waters to gauge my reaction. He didn't act because he saw my demeanor, sensed no fear, and could tell I wasn't going to cooperate. Also, the cart was between him and me and I could have used my bags or even the cart as a barrier between us. There may have been others in the lot watching and/or he may have seen me when I first went in.

Then she shared that she believed God was trying to raise my awareness because I had become too comfortable. I go to that grocery store almost every day at that time, thinking little of it. Although I'm very cautious, maybe I have become too comfortable. She said that several times. After I walked away from her office, all kinds of thoughts came to mind. God spoke through her and it gave me much on which to meditate.

First, it reminded me of the great, loving, protective shield, buckler and refuge I have in the Lord. That could have been a very bad day. I am extremely grateful to God for covering me, for not allowing anything to happen and for being my protector.

The Lord is my Shepherd… (See Psalm 23).

For He will give His angels charge over me to keep me in all my ways (See Psalm 91).

No weapon formed against me shall prosper… (See Isaiah 54).

The Lord shall preserve me from all evil; He shall preserve my soul (See Psalm 121).

His eye is on a sparrow and I know He watches me (See Matthew 10:29-31).

I ran across this verse fairly recently which says,

> *There is no one like the God of Jeshurun, who rides the heavens to help you…*
> –Deuteronomy 33:26a (NKJV)

And then, there is my favorite part of Deuteronomy 33:27a, which says,

> *The eternal God is thy refuge, and underneath are the everlasting arms:*

And 27b goes on with

> *He shall thrust out the enemy from before thee; and shall say, Destroy them."*

My Bible commentary says, "Like a soldier, the Lord is constantly on the lookout for ways to defend His people from attack. The Divine Warrior is always providing protection because He is eternal." But you won't know, understand or believe this if you are not consistent in reading the Word.

This got me to thinking about how consistency in prayer every day, ensures our covering. I plead the blood of Jesus over myself, my family, my friends, our ministry members and our church every day. And I know that others are doing the same for me. That is not something to take lightly—being covered by prayer. Are you covered? Husbands, are you covering your wives in prayer every day? Seriously, are you actually doing that?

What about covering your children? Mothers, are you covering your children? Again, do you actually plead the blood of Jesus over them before they start their day? And who's covering you? It is so important to start and set the tone of the day in thanksgiving and prayer, to declare how productive the day will be, and to cover yourself and others to keep weapons from prospering. To be sure, walking with the Lord does not mean that we will have a carefree life; no, that was never promised. In fact, we are told that in this world we will have trouble and that many are the afflictions of the righteous; but consistency in prayer and fellowshipping with the Lord each day, guarantees that we will have the Lord's presence, guidance and protection as we go through our days.

Our lives are not absent of trials or troubles, but I can honestly say that my life is absent of the kind of drama that unbelievers (and inconsistent believers) are burdened with. I think of some of the prayer requests our ministry has received and how many of those situational requests could be avoided first by being saved, and second by the added blessing of regular, consistent prayer in the lives of those requesting it. The Bible is full of promises for believers and we are in a covenant relationship. We maintain a full, abundant lifestyle with confession and repentance, praise and worship, thanksgiving, and consistent prayer.

The second thing that really stood out in what my co-worker told me was that "you've gotten too comfortable." That basically means you've let your guard down.

Be sober, be vigilant; because your adversary the devil, as a roaring lion, walketh about, seeking whom he may devour.
–1 Peter 5:8

The only way to do that is to be in prayer, hearing from the Lord. Inconsistency in prayer will dull your spiritual senses, cause you to lose momentum, get off track and necessitate having to start all over again.

So, I say to you, we cannot just coast through life, keeping God at bay, being inconsistent in prayer, not reading the Word and thinking that we will reap His benefits. It is only by His mercy that we stay as protected as we do. We must play our part and "work out our salvation with fear and trembling." I learned a lot from that incident in the parking lot. God covered me and kept me safe from harm, but it was also a warning not to get too comfortable and take things for granted. I am grateful for His covering, His wisdom, and His everlasting encouragement to remind me what's important and to do what I need to do to keep the momentum going. Beloved, cover yourself and your loved ones daily in prayer!

Takeaway Nugget: When you find yourself coasting in your spiritual life, start pedaling again!

Foundational Scripture: *Continue in prayer, and watch in the same with thanksgiving.*
–Colossians 4:2

Week 50

Lessons From My Blender

I was looking at my blender one morning while making a smoothie. I had put the fruit in it along with some water, and then turned it on. I wasn't facing the blender while it was on. When I looked back, I could see that the fruit was stuck. I wondered why nothing was happening. The power was on, but it wasn't moving yet. And the Holy Spirit began to speak to me. It's not time. Yes, the power is on, and the Holy Spirit is doing a work, but it just doesn't look like it.

I know it sometimes feels like you're waiting and nothing is happening. You and I may say, "I've cried and cried out, but nothing is moving. And then all of a sudden, I looked over at the blender and the fruit started moving." God is working. He's moving things into place. And while nothing appears to be moving, "nothing good is happening and nothing bad is happening," that's when God is saying,

> *"Be not weary in well doing for in due season, you will reap a harvest, if you faint not."*
> –Galatians 6:9

God is saying, "It's not time, I have to develop that fruit in you. Stay in the protective covering of the blender."

Think about how a blender is usually made of thick glass. It's deep and has a tight, sealed cover, so that the fruit doesn't get out before time and splash all over the place, possibly causing damage. Stay in the blender; abide while in the blender. God says, "I'm not working it out just for you; there are other people and circumstances that have to come into place." But then "suddenly" – and you don't determine the suddenly, God does – things start to churn, start to move and "blend" together, making something smooth, soft and refreshing!

Remember, the power (the Holy Spirit) was applied, but without Him, nothing moves except your flesh. He has to work on the fruit that's on the inside to stir things up and mesh others together. Once that is done, you're now ready to be poured out to minister to others, to help them get unstuck. After you've been poured out and the Lord uses you, remember to clean up right away. The blender has residue that sticks to the sides, so you have to wash it. Sometimes, the blender may require a bit of scrubbing because of those stubborn little seeds. Those are the things that He still needs to free you from. So, you must get washed again and again by reading the Word so that old residue doesn't cling to the surface. The longer you leave it, the harder it will be to remove it. So, wash immediately; don't let any time pass.

Stay in the Word every day. Stay in the blender for a while. The fruit is there; God just needs you to wait on Him. And then suddenly, when the time is right, you will be fresh and flourishing, ready to minister. You will be whole, blended, complete and even more beautiful than you are right now.

Takeaway Nugget: Don't get ahead of God. Abide with Him a while as He works on your character.

Foundational Scripture: *Wait on the LORD: be of good courage, and he shall strengthen thine heart: wait, I say, on the LORD.*

–Psalm 27:14

Week 51

Your Greatest Role

> "All the world's a stage, and all the men and women merely players; They have their exits and their entrances; And one man in his time plays many parts…"
> –Shakespeare, 1623/1936, p. 677

To a certain extent, he was right, but the truth is that we only have one role that really matters and it is important that we show up for it and act it out. Whether you realize it or not, as a child of God, you are an actor in the play of life, and your part has already been cast.

> *"For many are called, but few are chosen."*
> –Matthew 22:14

You were called for an audition and chosen for your role. Have you accepted the part? If so, this is what your spiritual career might sound like.

Depending on how well you've studied the script (the Bible), learned your lines (passages of Scripture), and obediently acted them out by being a doer of them and not just a hearer, determines whether or not you will win an Academy Award (the crown of life).

> *It is a good thing to give thanks unto the LORD, and to sing praises unto thy name, O Most High: To shew forth thy lovingkindness in the morning, and thy faithfulness every night.*
> —Psalm 92:1-2

So, as you give your acceptance speech, it is right to give thanks and praise to those who helped you. And your thanks might sound something like this:

"I would first like to thank my Father—my heavenly Father, Abba. I would like to thank my husbandman and my children. I thank our wonderful executive director, El Elyon; our producer, Jehovah Jireh; our make-up artist, Jehovah M'Kaddesh; our wonderful writer, Author and Finisher of our Faith; our music director, David; our lighting man, who we affectionately just call, The Light. I thank the other great supporters who worked behind the scenes: intercessors who prayed, tithers who donated the finances, seamstresses and tailors who provided the priestly garments, and all of you, the body of Christ, without whom all of us would not have made it because we know that lone rangers fail miserably.

And most of all, I want to thank my acting coach, the ultimate Helper—the Holy Spirit, who was with me every step of the way, encouraging me, teaching me, correcting me, guiding me, sustaining me and helping me with my lines by bringing them to my remembrance whenever I needed them."

Having said yes to the gift of salvation, it's been established that you've been called and chosen for your role. But the question is this: are you still waiting in the wings or have you accepted the role? If so, have you fully shown up for the part? God has given each of us a measure of faith and a specific purpose and destiny, having told us,

> *"For I know the thoughts that I think toward you, thoughts of peace and not of evil, to give you an expected end."*
> –Jeremiah 29:11

God has a part for you to play; one uniquely designed just for you; no one else can fulfill that role like you can. Before it's all said and done, we will have many roles—some dramas, some comedies and even tragedies, but they all have a purpose in growing your character so that you can be a blessing to someone else.

It's never about you; it's always about others. At the end of this journey, if you have performed well, if you have fought the good fight, run the race with perseverance, and played every part with passion, honesty, grace and authenticity; if you have given of your time and talent to others, perhaps to younger role players, training them up in the way they should go, then, prayerfully, you will find your name written in the Lamb's book of life, eligible to receive the Lifetime Achievement Award known as eternal life, where you will worship and praise the Lord forever!

To receive this award, though, you have to show up for your role now. It's urgent because you have a part to play now, for such a time as this! This is not a role you can turn down because it's a life and death matter. You have been uniquely selected, fearfully and wonderfully made for it. You are divinely equipped to successfully play it!

Some roles are small, and some are larger, but no matter the role you've been given, this is your greatest role. The time is now! Will you accept the part?

Takeaway Nugget: Great news...you got the part you auditioned for!

Foundational Scripture: *"For many are called, but few are chosen."*
–Matthew 22:14 (NKJV)

Week 52

Tell Them

Our greatest fear is not of heights or of water. It's not the fear of losing our jobs or a foreclosure. Nor is it fear of the dark or of spiders. It's not even public speaking, as many of us have been told. Our greatest fear is not being loved. We spend the majority of our days trying to look good, either physically or through accomplishments and performance. We strive at work; we dominate conversations, we grandstand, we try to obtain status, success or things so we can feel good about ourselves. We crave attention and try to ensure that the focus is on us, and why? All because we want to be accepted, approved of, praised, noticed, affirmed and validated. We want to be loved.

When we know that we are loved, we relax a little bit and feel more secure. Think of a person who loves you—someone who you know and believe really loves you. It could be a parent, a spouse, a relative or even a close friend. When we know that a person loves us (though that love is not, and can never be, perfect), we are more relaxed, content, and peaceful, and less likely to strive. There really is no need to strive. With that person, we don't have to be anything other than who we are. We don't try to prove anything, nor do we have to. We know that they just love us—our company, our personality, and just enjoy being with us. We really don't even have to talk or do anything special when we are with them; yet, our fellowship is sweet, and we look forward to being with that person. There is an aura of goodness and acceptance that emanates from them, and we just want to be near them. What emanates from them is plain and simply a feeling of being loved.

We are not afraid around them. There is no fear. Why? Because 1 John 4:18 NKJV tells us,

> *There is no fear in love; but perfect love casts out fear, because fear involves torment. But he who fears has not been made perfect in love.*

This is God's message to us. That's really all He wants us to know.

There is a movie called Joshua, which is about a representation of a modern-day Jesus. In one scene, Joshua has an audience with the pope, and this is what Joshua, representing Jesus, says to him:

"The world has become such a frightening place; there's so much anger and not enough love. Deep in the hearts of so many people, there's an emptiness that nothing of this world can fill and that emptiness makes it impossible for them to love."

"What should I do?" The pope asked.

"Remind them that I love them, that I died for them. Tell them that my love is real and if they open their hearts to it, I will fill that emptiness and they'll be able to love one another. That's the message; it hasn't changed. Tell them. Tell them."

God has been telling you and is telling you now that He loves you. As my pastor has written, "you are a fine, rare and precious stone to be cherished, loved and handled very carefully and tenderly as someone who is special." (Tyler, 2015, p. 77).

God tells you all throughout the Bible, which is His love letter to you, that you are loved. Listen to how He speaks of those who belong to Him:

He calls you beloved, apple of My eye, little flock, My sheep, little children.

Yea, I have loved thee with an everlasting love: therefore with lovingkindness have I drawn thee.
–Jeremiah 31:3b

"And if I go and prepare a place for you, I will come again, and receive you unto myself; that where I am, there ye may be also."
–John 14:3

Can a woman forget her nursing child, And not have compassion on the son of her womb? Surely, they may forget, Yet I will not forget you. See, I have inscribed you on the palms of My hands;
–Isaiah 49:15-16a (NKJV)

"I will not leave you comfortless: I will come to you."
–John 14:18

Fear not: for I have redeemed thee, I have called thee by thy name; thou art mine.
–Isaiah 43:1b

I will never leave thee, nor forsake thee.
—Hebrews 13:5b

"And I will give unto thee the keys of the kingdom of heaven:"
—Matthew 16:19a

I will strengthen thee; yea, I will help thee; yea, I will uphold thee with the right hand of my righteousness.
—Isaiah 41:10b

God loves you. Discover it. Believe it. Receive it. Embrace it. Live in it.

The love of Jesus is available to you today, right here, right now! If you have accepted Him as Savior and Lord and are walking righteously, love is all around you. Love is inside of you, love is in His Word, love is His Word. Love is in your heart, love is in stillness, love is timeless. Love is ageless, love is intimate, love is personal, love is real and love is offered freely and eternally to you. Receive it.

If you have not confessed Him as Savior and Lord, you can do so today by praying the following prayer or one similar to it: "

Heavenly Father, I come to You acknowledging that I am a sinner in need of Your forgiveness. I believe that Jesus Christ died on the cross for my sins and rose again. I confess Jesus as my Lord and Savior, and I invite Him into my heart to reign and rule over my life. Thank You for Your love, grace and forgiveness. In Jesus' name, I pray. Amen!

If you prayed the prayer sincerely from your heart, the next step is being discipled into the faith. You have asked Jesus into your heart. He immediately changed it and has accepted you, but you must now be taught how to live the life of a Christian. You must learn and grow into your salvation. It's not enough just to pray that prayer and continue with your old life. You have been translated into a new life and you must come into the fullness of that new life. To do that, you have to be taught.

Tell a mature Christian that you have prayed this prayer and ask them to help you continue the process by helping you find a Bible-believing, Holy Spirit-led Christian church that believes in all three persons of the Trinity [Father, Son (Jesus) and the Holy Spirit]. That church must believe that Jesus was born of a virgin, died on a cross on Calvary, was buried, rose three days after, ascended into heaven, and is seated at the right hand of the Father. They must also believe in the third person of the Trinity: the Holy Spirit. If you do not follow up with these steps, you have just stated some words and are no more saved and in a relationship with the Lord Jesus than a paper clip. You must be discipled into the faith or you will not have an abundant life here on earth nor eternal life once you die.

One of the greatest deceptions that occurs when people just pray this prayer is that they think that's all they have to do. It's not. Sadly, there is an inordinate number of people who believe they are saved, but they're not. So, do not be deceived or let others deceive you by telling you that just praying this prayer brings salvation.

It doesn't. You must go deeper and allow yourself to be mentored, so to speak. I implore you, with all heartfelt seriousness, to be discipled into your salvation. It will be the best gift you have ever received!

Takeaway Nugget: The God who created the universe and everything in it wants a personal relationship with you!

Foundational Scripture: *"Yea, I have loved thee with an everlasting love: therefore, with lovingkindness have I drawn thee."*
–Jeremiah 31:3b

Conclusion

Reflections for Abundant Life, A Spiritual Devotional, Practically Speaking was written to help you maintain or build a personal relationship with God through His Son, Jesus Christ! God loves you and wants you to know that you can know Him and live a full, abundant life.

Through each devotional in this book, you have been provided with information, spiritual and practical insights, and tools to help you build or maintain an intimate relationship with the Lord, Jesus Christ. It is my hope that you have been encouraged, inspired and provided with answers that will help you put your trust in Jesus and live out your faith with confidence. Be well! Be blessed!

For information on other books and how to purchase a wonderful set of affirmation cards created to encourage you on your journey, visit my website.

If you would like to reach out, I would love to hear from you.

With the love of Jesus,
Audrey

Website: CrossWordsDesigns.com
Email: contact@crosswordsdesigns.com

References

Week 3: Please Listen Carefully, as Our Menu Options Have Changed

Tyler, Lois. The Reconciled Church, 2017

Week 14: I Just Don't Know What to Think

Allen, James, *As Man Thinketh,* James Allen, 1903.

Week 20: Knock, Knock. Who's There?

Roper, D. (1994). *Psalm 23: The Song of a Passionate Heart.* Discovery House.

Week 32: Reclaiming What's Yours

Copeland, G. (2005), *Prayers that avail much.* Harrison House.

Week 45: The Six Million Dollar Man

Caidin, M. (Creator) (1974-1978). *The Six Million Dollar Man* [TV series]. Universal Television.

Week 48: What's Christmas to You?

Laurie, Greg. "What's Christmas to You?" *harvest., 25 December 2019, https://harvest.org/resources/devotion/what-christmas-is-about-6/*

Week 51: Your Greatest Role

Shakespeare, W. (1936). *As You Like It* (William Aldis Wright, Ed). Doubleday Doran & Co., Inc., (Original work published 1623).

Week 52: Tell Them

Joshua. Directed by Jon Purdy, Performances by Tony Goldwyn and Giancarlo Giannini, Epiphany Films and Crusader Entertainment LLC, 2002.

Tyler, L. (2015). Prayers of Abounding Faith. Daughters of Zion Ministries.

Made in the USA
Coppell, TX
03 July 2026

83443246R00154